THE
PARENT
AS
COACH®
APPROACH

THE
PARENT
AS
COACH®
APPROACH

THE 7 WAYS TO COACH YOUR TEEN
IN THE GAME OF LIFE

DIANA STERLING

WHITE OAK PUBLISHING
Albuquerque, New Mexico

Printed in the United States of America

Library of Congress Data Block

Sterling, Diana
    The PARENT as COACH® Approach: The Seven Ways to Coach Your Teen in the Game of Life by Diana Sterling
        p. cm.
    ISBN 978-0-9702255-2-8

    1. Parenting -- Social Aspects -- United States 2. Family --
    United States 3. Nature nurture

I. Sterling, Diana. II. Title
HQ755.h

Library of Congress Card Number: 2008932087

White Oak Publishing
A Division of New Generations International
4111 Barbara Loop SE, Suite E-1
Rio Rancho, New Mexico 87124

Website: www.parentascoach.com
Email: support@parentascoach.com

Edited by Nancy Osa
Book Design by Machele Brass
Cover Photo by Kal Yee

First Edition July 2008
First Printing

This book is printed on recycled paper.

CONTENTS

A MESSAGE TO PARENTS

If you **RESPECT** me,
I will hear you.

If you **LISTEN** to me,
I will feel understood.

If you **UNDERSTAND** me,
I will feel appreciated.

If you **APPRECIATE** me,
I will know your support.

If you **SUPPORT** me as I try new things,
I will become responsible.

When I am **RESPONSIBLE**,
I will grow to be independent.

In my **INDEPENDENCE**,
I will respect *you* and love *you* all of my life.

Thank you, Your Teenager

FORWARD AND ONWARD

Dear Readers,

I am a simple every day mom. I raised my son as a self-employed and self-supporting single parent. I had struggles. And....I found a new way to change the world when he was fourteen, but I learned that I first had to change me. So I set out to learn, to challenge myself, to grow, to ask hard questions of myself, to uncover my own gremlins and stare them in the face. I learned that I could change the paradigm of parenting I had been exposed to. I learned to be a parent as coach. The change in our relationship started with me.

So the Parent as Coach® journey began ten years ago in my own home. The first expression of this work came out in 2001 under the title, Parent as Coach. Now, seven years later Parent as Coach has become a household word around the world. I bring to you now, a re-titled version; The Parent as Coach Approach. The ideas, systems and The Seven Ways are all exactly as they have always been. In these past years that I have taken this work around the world, I have discovered that these perspectives are timeless and have no national borders, no language other than love, and no cultural boundaries. Therefore I have made no changes to how The Parent as Coach Approach works.

In the past seven years I have learned much, taught much, listened to the agonies of parents of teens, heard the desperate pleas from teens and young adults, cried with many, laughed with many, and seen the world over that something is not working. Kids are killing themselves, parents are having their out-of-control kids taken away in the night, families are in shreds, teachers in our education systems are exhausted, juvenile prisons and jails are overflowing, and school shootings have become practically every day headlines. This toxic environment that we have created for our next generation has brought me to a new place of unrelenting devotion for changing the way things are.

And still, the insights and changes I have experienced have been in me.

Through being my own first client, I learned to love again and found the love of my life, Bill Sterling. I changed my last name from Haskins to Sterling, with great conviction and purpose. Bill challenges me to take this work to an even bigger arena. Imagine with me, if you will, working together to fill a stadium with young people who are feeling a sense of self-respect, listening to each other with curiosity, understanding cultural differences, supporting each other's dreams and goals, appreciating unique gifts and talents and these young people are feeling a sense of personal responsibility to be a positive light and are making courageous and independent choices to make the world a better place. Can you see it? I can and I will see it in my lifetime.

In the past seven years, I have met many such positive young people. When I ask them "How did you get here?" or "What makes you so switched on?" I get one answer in many forms: they tell me about the relationship with their parents. This is not rocket science.

Since Parent as Coach first came out, I and my team have grown this body of work and it is still growing. We are on the verge of something important. Parent as Coach actually IS working. We ARE making a difference. It is in the present. Our success stories in the back of this book reveal that something extraordinary is happening in a grass roots way. Parent as Coach Approach is for all of us on the ground. It is not a lofty, expensive, or complicated methodology. Respecting people and listening to them actually produces results of increased self-esteem and communication. This allows people to reach for their highest selves.

We stand at a crossroads. Young people are not the leaders of the future. They are the leaders of today. They have more economic power, more influence and more potential than any previous generation. They know how to use 21st century technology to get things done. We can support them in using their powerful voice for good, not destruction.

Share this book with others, listen to the audio book on your i-pod (if you are that cool) or get others to download the e-book on line at www.parentascoach.com. Get the word out.

Read on and join me and the thousands of families the world over who are discovering new ways to relate and communicate. Our kids can't wait.

Onward!

Diana Sterling

INTRODUCTION

"Adolescent" stems from the Latin "alere,"
which means to nourish or to grow.

THE TEEN YEARS

How well do you remember your teen years? Do you remember the driving need to belong, to find a sense of who you were, to find some form of approval and acceptance from others? You may have admired kids who showed a measure of confidence and said, "How can I get to be like them?" All of these things that you craved were meant to fill an underlying need that we as human beings all share: the need to find a sense of our own selves.

I remember those years. I also remember feeling very alone in my search for self. Perhaps that is why I ultimately became a certified personal effectiveness coach, to further my own quest while helping others chart courses for the future and find greater fulfillment and meaning in their lives. As my own son, Jordan, approached his teens, I began to wonder if there were some way that I could help *him* to grow in the coming years, to lessen the loneliness and confusion that I had felt at his age. I came to realize that by applying my coaching skills to parenting, I could do much to diminish my son's sense of isolation during the "searching" years. I could be the one to rework our connection, and I could help him to develop the confidence he needs to move out into the world on his own.

Think back to your teenage years. How much easier would your struggle for self-identity have been if the people who cared for you had worked from the premise of your fundamental self-worth and dignity, rather than one of "guilty until proven innocent"? Now apply that concept to the teenagers you know.

By adjusting our job description as parents to include the active role of coach, we can create a space for our children to safely explore their own sense of self, and help them begin to find meaning in who they are and what they do. This can lay a foundation of mutual respect and trust on which to build eventual, ongoing adult-to-adult relationships. To achieve this, we must first approach our teenagers from this basic standpoint: that they are good, and worthy of our love, respect, time, and attention.

FINDING A NEW APPROACH

So the idea for *Parent as Coach* developed in my own home. When my son and his friends reached their preteens, I noticed them engaging in new behaviors like grunting, hunching over, and alternately ignoring me when I spoke to them or responding in one-syllable sentences or being critical—you get the picture. I would say to them, "Oh, I see you're practicing for your teenage years!"

One day my son asked me why I made such derogatory remarks about teenagers, and how come every time he did something I didn't approve of I'd say it must be a "teenager" thing. He accused me of labeling him: "You are like all the other adults I know—critical and hard on teenagers," he said. "You think we are all broken and bad!"

Again he questioned my motives, and I have to admit I found myself fumbling for the "right" answer. I finally saw that, indeed, I had been making presumptions about what was true for all teens. I also realized that my son saw through to the heart of the matter, and that he was right. Why did I hold onto the casual notion that being a teenager was synonymous with "bad"?

I explored my hidden assumptions about teens and decided to discuss them with my son. I asked him for his side of the story. After some real heart-to-heart talks, I came to the obvious conclusion: that, in his own way, this young person was asking me, the adult, for the opposite of what I was doing. My son was asking me to see him and his peers as positive, creative, searching, developing, wonderful individuals, not as a band of aliens from outer space. He didn't want to be prejudged or disregarded, he wanted to feel respected and heard. He didn't want me to be ambivalent or remote, he wanted me to be a positive force for him, and consistently there with him during this time of inner and outer changes.

I began to experiment with a different approach. I started interacting with my son in a way that honored him for exactly who and where he was at that point in time. After all, I figured, fourteen is tough enough without your parent chiming in about what's wrong with you and what's wrong with teenagers in general all the time. I started using different vocabulary, stopped rolling my eyes at his "antics." I began to see him differently, complete in all of his complexities and insecurities. And I began to treat him differently as I adjusted something in *me*.

I wondered if I could stay true to my parenting commitment while my son naturally asserted more independence. Could I meet his need for separation without counterwithdrawal? Was there a way to still nurture and guide him without becoming anxious and oppressive? I contemplated parenting this young man through a conscious, positive attitude and loving support, rather than just holding my breath and hoping for the best for the next six to seven years.

I let these new possibilities simmer in my mind, and imagined myself as my son's coach in the game of life. I began to see myself as a parent-coach.

At about the time my son and I were having these new types of conversations, I had the opportunity to work with thirty other teens in a one-on-one coaching situation at a local high school. In addition to college- and career-based questions, I asked each of them the following:

- What do you need from adults in the teen years?
- How do you want to be treated by parents and other adults?
- How do you want to live your life in the future?
- What can you do to find meaning in your life?

I discovered that teenagers want and need to be asked these questions. Some had tears in their eyes at the simple notion that they could actually find purpose in their lives—and that they could design a way of life that is both joyful and meaningful. When asked if they thought adults could help them in this endeavor, most were skeptical. Sixteen-year-old Mary Beth stated the problem best:

"In society today, teenagers receive little to no respect from adults. In stores, we're always being followed, watched, and suspected of shoplifting. Sure, there are rowdy kids who give the rest of us a bad name, but it's not fair that adults pigeonhole us and place us under a stereotype that damages the way that everyone views our generation.

"Many teenagers act out and rebel due to lack of respect from their parents. If my parents don't show me respect, how do you think that will make me feel? Useless? Less than? Like I don't deserve to be respected?

"If my parents, my two essential role models in life, don't respect me, how can I respect myself? How can I plan the rest of my life if no one respects who I am now?"

And so I delved deeper.

I looked at the other half of the equation: the adults. In interviewing over one hundred adults, I asked, "What is the first word that comes to mind when you think of a teenager?" Most told me without hesitation: *lazy, irresponsible, sloppy, rebellious, confused, adversarial, selfish, moody, stubborn, demanding, insecure, aloof, unpredictable . . .*

Did all adults think that all teenagers were like this? There had to be a reason for such common negative impressions of teens by the adults in their lives. I asked adults, "Do you sometimes fear teenagers? Are you frustrated with them and let them know it? Do you avoid them whenever possible?" The answer was almost always yes to all of these questions. Many parents added stories of how family dynamics had changed once their kids hit the teen years, and of their own feelings of overwhelm, exhaustion, disappointment, heartache, and despair. I knew I had to somehow find a way to help.

Again I returned to my own experience. I knew that if any change in the parent-teen relationship were to be possible, the recipe must include me, the adult, taking responsibility to reshape the way I *think* about teenagers.

So I hit the books. I went back to the basics to learn more about the mental and physical development of the child over the first twenty-one years of life. I discovered that in the teen years, marked by the onset of puberty and physical transition into adulthood, major changes take place in a child's thought processes. New cognitive capacity allows a teen to accomplish more complex mental and physical tasks, and to seek and establish new self-motivated routines. This is an unparalleled time of development—of seeking, learning, experimenting, and facing new hurdles and opportunities. Add these challenges to the world we live in and the warp speed at which we often live our lives . . . These are scary times, enough to make any young person feel uncertain. I wondered just where I fit into the whole scenario.

I had come full circle, back to where I'd begun, with memories of me as a teen myself, alone in my search for an identity. How could adults be a part of teens' lives when the relationship seemed impossible or at best, difficult? Fortunately, another teenager I knew would provide an answer.

I asked Stephen, a twenty-year-old client, to look back on his recent teen years and share with me his one essential message for parents and adults. He said simply, "Be there. Don't leave us."

I asked him to explain.

"When we're little," he said, "parents see kids as close companions, come to our soccer games, make our lunch, and things like that. But when we get to be teenagers, they think we can manage it all on our own, and they withdraw into their busy lives. I would say to parents, *don't leave us*, because we still need you."

I finally concluded that it is us, the adults, who hold the key. If teens ask, adults must answer—even if we don't have the "right" answer. And when they *don't* ask, we must remain steady at the helm. We can do more than just "fix what's broken" or "make it through the day" with our kids. We are the ones who must keep the connection alive, through consistent, active, and loving parenting, in order to form healthy relationships with our teenage children. We have that power.

Teenagers who react to the growth period by behaving alternately distant and then "in your face" are doing exactly what they are supposed to be doing at this age. They are doing their jobs by testing, exploring, questioning, pushing the envelope. They are surrounded by opportunities (and temptations) to pursue new interests and try new things. And in the middle of it all, they don't want to lose the bond with parents and other adults—they just want to modify it, and this is the natural order of things. Though they must go on to make their own lives, teenagers are loudly and clearly asking us to participate with them.

COACHING YOUR TEEN

Who coached or mentored you? Was there someone who made a difference in your life when you were young? Many people recall one very special adult; some claim no one. Which legacy will you pass on? Whether acting as a parent or a concerned elder, you have the opportunity to be the one to guide a teenager in the search for a meaningful life. But how?

The formula is complex, yet simple: If we respond to the needs of teens, they will respond to us. The first step is to take the "I" out of our sentences and actions—what *I* would do, how *I* once handled things—and see things through the eyes of young people.

We must appreciate their unique points of view no matter how fragile or bold, tentative or insistent they (or we) may be. And we must acknowledge their ideas no matter how tired, frustrated, or overwhelmed we may feel at the time. These are the tasks of the parent-coach.

In working with teenagers and listening to their views, I saw seven themes emerge, seven "requests" of the adults in their lives. In order to keep communication open and stay connected, **teens want adults to**:

> **RESPECT** them;
> really **LISTEN** to them;
> **UNDERSTAND** their points of view;
> **APPRECIATE** their specialness;
> **SUPPORT** them with love and kindness;
> promote new levels of **RESPONSIBILITY**;
> and nurture their unfolding **INDEPENDENCE**.

By actively addressing each of these areas, the parent-teen relationship becomes a two-way street rather than a dead end.

These seven requests form the basis for the parent-coach approach. As you read this book, allow me to coach *you* as you begin to imagine yourself coaching the young person in your life. I'll introduce you to practical methods for forming new habits that will open up a whole new way of being with your teenager. You'll read personal stories from parents and young adults of diverse backgrounds that will illuminate your own situation and let you proceed from a new vantage point. Using your new coaching perspective and skills as building blocks, you will lay the foundation for powerful connection and communication with your teenager that will sustain you both during the inevitable stormy periods ahead. By nourishing your teen through the role of coach, your relationship can surpass anything that has gone on before.

Though you may see some changes in yourself or your child right away, *Parent as Coach* is not a quick-fix, nor is coaching a one-size-fits-all endeavor. Use this book as a tool kit in your ongoing mission to improve or sustain the connection with your teen or preteen. Keep a notepad handy or scribble in these margins. Track your progress and ideas, what does and doesn't work for you. Keep on learning, and share your findings with your spouse or with other parents. Tell the world!

Begin by trying on the role of coach in Part One, "Becoming a Parent-Coach." Learn the *why* of teens' changing behavior, and how to enhance the qualities and skills you already possess.

Put your new skills to work in Part Two, "Seven Ways to Coach Your Teen." Each of the Seven Ways corresponds to a call and a response—your teenager's need, or call, and your response. As your coach, I provide practice exercises to help you arrive at an effective approach for your individual family situation.

Don't expect to "finish" any or all of these practice exercises. The word *practice* denotes continued learning and commitment; it is something that continues over a lifetime, often unassociated with closure or completion. Feel free to adapt these suggestions to suit your particular style, and keep on trying until you arrive at a way that fits.

In Part Three, "Coaching Questions Parents Ask," read about the situations that other parents face and how the *Parent as Coach* method can help. Some of these questions might sound familiar!

When you step into the role of parent-coach, you will easily recall your own teen years, your hopes and fears, your tests and triumphs. You'll know that you and your teenage child are but two parts of a living, breathing whole—the continuum of life. You will have made the choice to explore the possibilities of this young person's life together, to find the best way for her or for him to grow with courage, confidence, and compassion—and to pass those qualities on to future generations.

PART ONE:
BECOMING A PARENT-COACH

YOUR CHANGING ROLE

THE COACHING PERSPECTIVE

THE QUALITIES OF A COACH

THE SKILLS OF A COACH

WHAT'S NEXT? TAKE ACTION!

PART ONE:
BECOMING A PARENT-COACH

1. YOUR CHANGING ROLE

Being a parent is a lifelong commitment that begins with the birth of a child and lasts through all phases of life. As our children change and grow, what do we as parents do to evolve with them? We can't stand still. While the primary *relationship* remains the same, the *role* needs to change for the parent as the child develops. Imagine yourself passing through three distinct phases, or parenting roles, over the course of the first twenty years of your child's life:

Think of your first role during the formative years of the young child (approximately 0-6 years) as PARENT-TEACHER. You are your child's first contact with mental and physical learning. You literally spend thousands of hours together in day-to-day activities, feeding, rocking, reading, and playing. It is a time of physical intensity in response to the child's need. It is a time of nurturing.

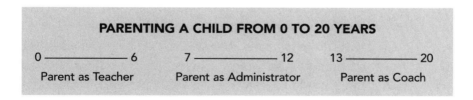

PARENTING A CHILD FROM 0 TO 20 YEARS

0 ——————— 6	7 ——————— 12	13 ——————— 20
Parent as Teacher	Parent as Administrator	Parent as Coach

At about six or seven years of age, the mental transition from "learning to read" to "reading to learn" has occurred, and the child can begin to absorb information independently. In the middle years (roughly 7-12), your child begins to initiate activities and create social groups, and needs an adult to help organize events and provide transportation, among many other supportive functions. Without completely abandoning your role as parent-teacher, you take on the additional role of PARENT-ADMINISTRATOR—managing your child's schedule and enabling him to explore his growing interests.

In the early teen years, as mentioned in the Introduction, a child's intellectual process expands with new capability for abstract thought. As your child begins to manage her own scheduling and decision making, you may be fired from your role as administrator on the spot. Then what? Your job as parent goes on, but the role you play must change. At this point, you must make a conscious decision: Continue to monitor homework, nag about picking up clothes, meet your teen's silence with your frustration—or accept nature's changes and take on the role of PARENT-COACH.

By the time my son reached fourteen or fifteen, he had developed into a full-fledged teenager, physically and mentally. One evening as we prepared to settle in for the night, I said to him, as I had for the past twelve years or so, "Don't forget to brush your teeth!"

He replied quite plainly, "Mom, you don't have to tell me that anymore. I have that managed."

I was in the process of being fired as administrator, but did not yet know how to be a coach. I thought about it awhile, and realized that if I wanted to continue being involved in my son's life, I would have to find a new way of interacting with him, other than the administrator mode I'd grown used to. Otherwise, I would be doomed to become a nag, interrogator, and maybe even spy.

I also sensed that my son wanted me to trust him to have those little things handled, so that we could trust each other enough to communicate about the bigger things that would soon come up, like curfew, driving, or dating. He seemed to be asking me to be ready for the bigger issues.

Our way of being together was about to come to an end, and in order to maintain a communicative relationship, I would have to adapt. Later, I realized that I was not alone. All parents face these changes. If we want the opportunity to mentor, guide, and support our teenage children through this phase of their lives, we must alter—not abandon—our parenting style. We must become parent-coaches.

So, get ready. When your child makes the shift into the teenage years, it is time for your role to shift as well. Though you may think you've arrived at a parenting plateau—your child's physical needs have lessened and she is taking on more responsibility—you find you have to change your ways, and you may not be ready to do so. During this evolution, stay committed to your long-term parenting relationship, and *allow your role to change.*

Begin early, if you can, during the preteen years. Examine your own values and actions, so you will be ready when your soon-to-be teenager experiments with hers. This will allow you to become grounded and centered in who you are as a parent. As you navigate the intricacies of close bonding and immanent separation, think about where you would like to be in your growing child's life, and ask yourself, "How am I going to parent now? Where can I find support, and what new things must I learn?"

NOTES

★

2. THE COACHING PERSPECTIVE

So, as you and your teenager evolve together, the role of coach rewards both of you during this time of discovery and transition. To understand how, imagine an Olympic athlete up on a platform, receiving a medal. On the sidelines stands you, the coach. You have trained, mentored, taught, cheered, cried, and laughed while nurturing the young athlete toward the accomplishment of a dream. The goal of winning was the athlete's, but together you worked toward that goal.

The moment of glory is all about the athlete's commitment, dedication, and achievement. You were there to evoke a level of excellence and performance not in yourself, but in the young person. In the ideal coaching relationship, the athlete does not become dependent on you, the coach, but goes on with greater confidence and courage to manage other areas of sports and life.

The same progression holds true for the parent-coach. A coach is not just a cheerleader, but one who helps an individual explore his or her potential and supports them in moving on to bigger and better things. Without a coach, some may falter or give up. Your job as parent-coach is to give your teenager the support and the means to strive toward a full life, even after you step aside.

So what exactly does the parent-coach do for the teenager? For starters, we show our children that their ideas and viewpoints matter. This means listening deeply for where a young person is really coming from, supporting his interests, showing we appreciate her uniqueness. We do these things to help our children build a sense of self-worth and to help them find their true identities as individuals.

Then, how does the teenager benefit from the coaching relationship? What are the advantages of knowing that one's views,

that one's life, matters? The possibilities are endless. A healthy
and positive parent-teen relationship can allow teenagers:

- to find affirmation of their value as human beings;
- to mirror respect and appreciation;
- to learn the gentle courtesy of listening to others;
- to cultivate a desire to interact;
- to contemplate and form values and convictions;
- to learn when and how to negotiate and compromise;
- to want to extend themselves in a compassionate way with others;
- to feel an integral part of society;
- to embrace life's challenges.

Mark, a nineteen-year-old client, came to me because he wanted
to stop wandering aimlessly through college and wished to chart
a course. He told me that the only thing he knew that lay ahead
was a college degree (in anything), a meaningless job, a house in
the 'burbs, and a wife and a couple of kids. I asked him if that's
what he really wanted, and he seemed struck by the question.
"What do you mean, is that what I want?" he asked. "Isn't that
what I'm supposed to do?"

Over several months we explored what Mark was passionate
about, and then began to lay out a plan for his college and career.
He decided that the above-mentioned life was somebody else's
idea of happiness, and that what he wanted more than anything
was for his work to be meaningful and satisfying. For him the
goal was living each day to its fullest and contributing to society
in such a way that his life and work mattered to others.

As a coach, over time, I taught Mark that he had a choice in
the design of his life, that he didn't have to blindly follow along
with anyone else's program. I showed him how to clarify his

values, how to "choose to choose," how to take responsibility for his actions. I helped him build these inner resources so he could pursue his options and make conscious choices based on what was important to him. A parent-coach can do this, too.

Teenagers all over the world want meaning and purpose in their lives, just like you and me. Showing them that they are *worthy* of such a life is part of the coaching process—showing them how to give of themselves to attain it is the core of what coaching is all about.

NOTES

★

3. THE QUALITIES OF A COACH

Who are you? Do you know? The most important aspect of being a coach is *knowing yourself*. If you are setting out to help your teen in his search for identity, you had better examine your own life first. As you ask more of your teen in your position as coach, be true to yourself, and let it show. Walk the talk.

You already possess many of the qualities of a coach to some extent; you must now become aware of them and make them even more intentional. As you face each new situation with your teen:

SET AND REFLECT STANDARDS
that define your expectations;

BE FLEXIBLE AND CREATIVE
in how you uphold those standards;

HAVE PATIENCE
and remember the big picture; and

BE CONSISTENT
on all levels.

Setting Standards

What are your standards? What are your commitments? Do you keep your word? Are you devoted to a spiritual path or a course of lifelong learning? Do you strive for excellence in all areas, such as finances, work, partnerships, health? If these are the life goals we wish for our children, we must strive for them ourselves.

What does your child see when he looks to you as a role model? Teenagers have the insight and thought capacity to dissect the meaning of our actions. Because our motives may be unclear or we may downplay unpleasant aspects of our own characters, our teens ask us for explanations at every turn. *Why?* is a popular refrain.

Have you ever been held accountable by a teenager to be true
to your word or to follow through on something you said you'd do?
It is a humbling experience, that's for sure! As parents, we set the
bar high for our kids. As coaches, we must remember to raise our
own bars and lead by example.

Being Flexible and Creative

Our standards and values do not exist in a vacuum. While
upholding our standards, we must be able to adapt to a changing world, and more importantly, *a changing teenager*. Have you
noticed? Just when you think you've got it all dialed, you get a
busy signal, or an outright disconnect. You have to go back to
the basics, and reevaluate yourself and your methods. I call this
staying LIQUID in the process of parenting teenagers.

We must also be open to reshaping our expectations over time.
Developmentally, all teens will be different from one year to
the next. That's their biological job. So, keep your options open;
things can and will change. A high-school junior or senior facing
graduation soon will respond much differently to a conversation
about college than will a freshman. Our job as parents is to stay
fluid through these years.

Being flexible celebrates the uniqueness of your teen. I know a
family that has a set of twins, both currently in high school. The
two teens attend different schools in order to give them both the
chance to excel in their very different learning styles. Their parents have set a goal for homework completion, knowing that the
twins have different rhythms when it comes to getting the homework done. They wisely allow some flexibility in when and how
it gets done, to accommodate each one's capabilities. Remember
that while the destination may be the same for all, there are
many ways to get there.

Having Patience

Some of us are patient by nature; others must work at it, remind-
ing and re-reminding ourselves of the big picture. When you feel
yourself losing patience, find a way to *pause* inside, and reflect.

Patience is a long-term investment. Helping your precious teenager build a life for the future takes time!

Your teen may not reinforce this concept. In these days of computers, cell phones, video games, and online shopping, young people have been brought up to think that all of life can run at Internet speed. It is up to you to remember that your relationship with your child goes on, day after day, past the teen years and into adulthood. Patience will reward you with a truly interactive relationship over the years. That is the prize.

Even though your teen may seem to be hard-wired to the speed of her video games and computers, she can only grow and learn in *biological* time. That is, we learn only at the speed with which our physical bodies can actually assimilate new information. Have reverence for this miracle, and let it guide you toward patience with your daughter.

Liken this experience to riding a bike. Did you jump on a bike at five years of age and immediately begin to sail down the street? No, you learned it over time, fitting each piece of information about riding a bike into your mind and into your body. You fell and got up, fell and got up. After much learning and practice, you now ride a bike like a master. As you and your teen learn new things from the coaching perspective, keep your feet firmly on the pedals, allow yourself to lean on the training wheels when you have to, and be patient without demanding extreme results right away.

In shifting your way of being to one as parent-coach, remember to have patience with yourself as well. The skills that follow in this book, while learnable, are not finite, and neither is your teen's personality. Give yourself permission to get familiar with these new ways of relating with your teen gradually, letting them unfold in your mind, your heart, and your body. Take one new idea at a time, and practice, practice, practice. And take comfort in small changes: You're learning.

By working from a foundation of patience, all of a parent-coach's practice pays off—in small dividends paid out regularly over a lifetime.

Being Consistent

Consistency is a wellspring to return to when faced with the day-to-day changes in the world and in your teen. When you are consistent in your actions, and when your words match your deeds, your teen will absorb this pattern and be able to act consistently himself. Won't that be a big help in getting the homework done?

Consistency also means being available to your teen on a regular basis. Being busy and overworked or overwhelmed is the reason many parents give for not "being there" for their kids who are now physically capable of taking care of themselves. Parents admit that intense work, travel, and personal schedules—once manageable back in the day care and baby-sitter years—become crazy-making and intolerable when kids hit their teens. Those teenagers who are left alone, virtually abandoned to video games and fast food, have no choice but to fend for themselves in any way they can.

Contrary to being self-sufficient, children approaching the teen years need an *increased* level of parental involvement. This is actually the time for parents to slow down and consider limiting their own outside activities. One parent describes this phenomenon as the shift from a need for "quality time" to "quantity time."

Add up in your mind the actual hours and minutes that you are physically available to your teen. If necessary, rework your schedule—take work home, find a new indoor hobby, invite friends to your place. Teenagers want to know that you're home. Think about what your child is asking for: *"Be there. Don't leave us."*

NOTES

4. THE SKILLS OF A COACH

Now that you are consciously focusing on your qualities as coach, you are ready to pick up the more tangible tools of coaching. Start by observing yourself as you interact with your teen. **Do you:**

SPEAK
clearly?

LISTEN TO UNDERSTAND
your teen's point of view?

STAY OPEN
to possibilities?

RESERVE
your judgments?

FOCUS
on outcomes?

These are the real building blocks of good relationships. As you focus on these actions, you'll come to recognize your own habits and be able to modify them accordingly.

Don't worry if these new behaviors seem strange. Keep trying! Soon, using these skills will be second nature to you, and your teen will come to rely on them.

Speaking

Speech is an influential tool, with the power to uplift, support, or guide as well as to hurt, tear down, or abuse. It is often used carelessly, as a reflex action. Remember to think and breathe before you speak. Be conscious of how you use this double-edged sword.

The act of speaking involves *word choice* plus *delivery*. Let's dissect the way we speak to our kids. Our choice of words must convey real respect, rather than grudging tolerance. Our delivery—a combination of breath, vocal tone, cadence, and body posture—must correspond to our words, or all meaning is lost. "Empty" words, those not backed up by positive delivery, are akin to a smile on the lips but not in the eyes. We all know that that person doesn't really mean what he or she is saying.

Observe yourself and how you speak to your teen. Is your overall tone one of civility and respect, or are your words tight and edgy, conveying impatience and frustration? Is your language positive and encouraging, or is it peppered with negatives springing from the unspoken assumption that all teens are difficult, irresponsible, and rebellious?

Try this: Ask a friend or partner for some thoughts on how you speak in your teen's presence. Ask these questions: Do I speak in a way that invites my teen to open up and talk to me? Do I use the word *should* in telling him what to do, implying that I know exactly the right way to behave? What are my trip-up spots—what causes me to lose control and say things I'll regret that may hurt his self-esteem?

Consciously take control of your words and manner of speaking. Vocalize *clear requests*. If your son or daughter is not doing what you ask or not honoring boundaries in the household, it may be because they don't really know where you stand on a matter or what you actually want of them. Take a mental inventory and assess whether your requests are clear enough.

For instance, a client named Andrea became frustrated when her son David wouldn't wash the dinner dishes in a timely manner. She'd say to him, "I would really like it if you would do the dishes after dinner." He would make no response, and Andrea would angrily attack him, demanding after the fact, "Why aren't the dishes done?"

At my suggestion, she made a clear request of her son, asking him to set a time frame. She said to David, "Since it is your night to do the dishes, what time would you like to start?" Amazed at the result, Andrea reported: "He said, 'Okay, in ten minutes I'll start the dishes.' No battles, no fighting, he just did them!"

In making a clear request and receiving acknowledgment, you have made an *agreement* with your teen. Agreements can be made about small things like dishes or putting away clothes, or over larger issues. As adults, we make and keep agreements with colleagues and spouses every day in our work and home lives. We don't expect them to read our minds. Shouldn't we extend this practice to our teenagers, rather than assuming that they know what we want and expect?

Another parent named Carolyn uses agreements as a separate "language" to cut down on hazardous assumptions. "If I ask my son Michael to put the garbage out on Monday nights, I ask in a specific way and I know what we are agreeing to," she relates. "I have learned not to assume that if I ask him one time, he will automatically adopt the responsibility each week. I have to decide what I'm asking for and be clear in my request, such as, 'Will you take out the garbage every week on Monday nights, and can we make an agreement that this is your ongoing responsibility?'"

By using the "agreement" word, Carolyn's expectations are stated clearly and precisely, and her son recognizes the need for a level of commitment on his part. Otherwise, he is left on his own to fill in the blanks, and may respond later with something that sounds like an excuse. "He now makes clear requests of *me*," says Carolyn, "and asks me to keep *my* agreements with him. Our language of agreements helps keep us both honest and accountable to keeping our word."

Getting into the habit of making agreements over little things like household chores will prepare you both to handle the larger matters, from driving to dating and beyond. This will prepare your emerging young adult to deal with all of life's later decisions.

"Do as I say" must be backed up with "do as I do." All children learn by example. The parent-coach must model the cause-and-effect relationship of agreements:

> **MAKE CLEAR REQUESTS**
> of others;
>
> **MEAN WHAT YOU SAY—**
> don't agree to things you're uncomfortable with
> or won't really accomplish.
>
> **KEEP YOUR WORD;**
>
> **LET YOUR TEEN SEE YOU FOLLOW THROUGH**
> with what you said you would do!

Listening

Actively listening for a young person's point of view is vital. Listening is the key to understanding, and teenagers in search of an identity yearn to be understood. Are you tuning into your teen in a way that allows her to really feel heard? Do you listen deeply and quietly, or do you tend to "step on her lines" in an effort to provide a quick solution or "right" answer?

Slow down… and listen for where your teen is coming from. If you are only hearing her words and not what lies beneath, you create a distance. Take a breath when she talks to you, and avoid interpreting how *you* might handle something. Remember that the coaching focus is not on *you*. Rather than counseling what your teen should do, listen for what she could do. Ask her opinion, acknowledge her unique ideas, invite real discussion. Our teenage children are not perfect duplicates of us, they are *themselves*. Honor who they are, and who they are becoming.

A client, Michelle, told me she'd recently been "blasted" by her nineteen-year-old daughter, Jennifer. This young woman was harshly critical and told her mother that she did a lousy job of parenting, and that she was going to live her life quite differently from now on, thank you very much! Michelle was obviously heart-broken and distressed at having engaged in a terrible and sad fight, but could only defend herself to me, saying that she'd done a good job raising her daughter, and that this was the thanks she got.

It struck me how truly sad it was that this mother could not hear anything or respond from the perspective of this young woman in search of herself—the daughter whom she loved so much. Perhaps if the two had established early on that they might not always agree on values and lifestyles, but would try to honor each other's opinions and expressions, the big blast might have been managed differently. Had they developed a deeper way of listening, they may have been able to take a moment to see the other's point of view.

It is no small task to debate basic core values with one's offspring, but we do have a choice in how we respond to them. Try listening with an open heart, and start when they are young. Set out to improve your listening skills with the goal of stepping into the young person's point of view. **Listen:**

FOR THE ROOT
of what teens are saying;

FOR WHAT THEY ARE NOT SAYING;

TO THEIR DELIVERY
as well as their words;

TO UNDERSTAND,
not just to react;

WITH COMPASSION.

Staying Open

Coaching teenagers is not a finite science; it's about trying new things, sharing ideas, and making suggestions. Having a rigid formula by which you coach all teenagers will get you nowhere. *Remain open* to new ways of doing things. Return to your basic coaching qualities: remember the importance of setting standards, being flexible, having patience, and acting consistently. Remind yourself that parenting is an open-ended process.

Staying open shows that you are willing to stick with your teen through the ups and downs of life. Recognize that each individual child will experience life differently—not the way you did, nor the way his brothers and sisters did. This mindset allows the teenager the freedom to find his own style. Parents with more than one child tell me that they can be as consistent and firm as they wish, but to be effective they find they must adapt to each one's learning style and blossoming personality.

My client Jeff, a highly competitive former football player, learned firsthand how to let his son reach his own conclusions about competition. Jeff's son, Ryan, enjoys rock climbing, so Jeff enrolled him in a gym in their neighborhood in order to practice. Meanwhile, another gym invited the young man to join its junior rock-climbing team in competitions. Father and son researched the competitive aspects of the sport, and Ryan attended several team practices.

On the day of his first scheduled competition, Ryan told his father that he'd decided not to participate. He explained that climbing was more of a recreational sport for him, and that competing was not his goal. Jeff kept quiet and let him talk awhile, not expressing his own strong opinions on competition. He allowed his son to resolve the decision about the team on his own. Jeff refrained from giving advice or pressuring his son in any way, empowering him to make the choice. And he did—Ryan's exact words were: "I choose not to go today and compete. I am choosing to be a recreational rock climber."

★

Coaching is not about handing out the right answer, but about preparing teenagers to make their own choices. Sometimes advice is needed when teens approach adults with a situation or problem, but more often gentle guidance through the process of discovery will benefit a young person more. Rather than trying to solve every problem, we must learn to listen and speak in such a way that allows young people to find some of their own answers.

Reserving Judgment

What do you do when your teenager: a) dabbles in a new discipline, from vegetarianism to meditation? b) gets to know someone from outside your social sphere? c) wants a tattoo or a nose ring? Of course you will have an opinion. Do you instinctively judge that which is different to be wrong or less than perfect? Do you articulate that judgment? Do you go on to criticize your teen before any real discussion has taken place?

Judging a teenager *when she is doing her job* and searching for answers can be very detrimental to your relationship. Remember your role as coach here, not administrator. Instead of defaulting to a judgmental attitude when your teen does or proposes something you don't like or don't approve of, try to engage her in a way that allows you to get the whole story. Learn what lies behind her needing or wanting something, or wanting to explore something out of her realm. This is how the parent-coach reserves judgment, changing an instinctual negative outlook to one that explores the possibilities.

My client Joe reported that he found a way to set his own interpretations aside and see a new perspective. His daughter Ann came to him with a heart-wrenching story of betrayal by a friend at school. "I saw this as an opportunity to keep *me* out of *her* story," he said.

With that in mind, Joe was able to pull back from recycling a quick solution that had worked for him in *his* youth. He was able to truly listen and to be with his daughter in an entirely new way. "I let her go through it and supported her in being brave. I hung out in her space. I listened and didn't judge her or the other girl. The result is that we were able to have a long discussion, and she felt heard and respected."

The more you can observe and assess the situation without flying off the handle, the more likely you are to have meaningful conversations with your teenager. If that sounds like an impossible dream, you have only to give this restraint a try.

Focusing on Outcomes

We live in the present, but we must look ahead to the future. When coaching clients, I'll often ask them to describe what result, or *outcome,* they are looking for down the road. Then I'll ask, "What would you do differently now in order to create what you want in the future?" We look ahead to the coming years and together focus on how to achieve the stated outcome.

The parent-coach must also keep the future in mind. As you talk, help your teenager imagine new prospects, and then follow through by supporting and helping him attain what it is he says he wants. Even if the attraction turns out to be fleeting and he loses interest, he will have learned that much more about himself: he isn't up to dog sledding, or he doesn't like playing with a band but does excel as a soloist. Recognizing the individuality of your teen and allowing him to search out meaning for himself is one of the most powerful gifts you can give. In coaching, we call this *designing a path toward a desired outcome.*

Jeff, whose son disclosed a love for rock climbing but not for competing, had an opportunity to support his teenager in moving forward as a recreational climber. By not interfering, he allowed his son to focus on what it was he really wanted. Being a parent-coach puts you in a position to help design a path toward a goal or outcome, giving your child the tools to fulfill dreams big and small.

In coaching teenagers, I inevitably get around to talking about college, careers, jobs, or any other post–high school plans with them. These are the big questions, and they can be scary. Many teens try not to think about them at all.

I teach these young people to see their next few decision-making years as an adventure. We start by considering what they want for the future—who and what and where they want to be. Then we work backwards to come up with a plan that will get them to that point. We literally draw on paper a big timeline, filling in anticipated milestones, such as S.A.T. tests, college or job applications, financial aid inquiries or resume writing, opening a checking account, finding a place to live, moving, etc. Through it all, there is *always* an end in mind, like a college degree or a job at a certain company or starting a business doing something they really love. We begin with the end in mind and make a map.

Note the *we* in this equation. Mapping out a teen's life *for her* doesn't work. That creates a dependency on you, the parent, to always do the planning, and doesn't take into account your daughter's unique hopes and dreams for life. Yet, staying totally out of the way and letting your teen navigate the intricacies of high school, college, and/or career planning leaves her feeling alone and unsure. By focusing on the big picture, you'll be able to strike a balance in your contribution to your teen's life that will be agreeable and comfortable for you both.

NOTES

★

5. WHAT'S NEXT? TAKE ACTION!

Now that you have assessed your current status as a parent and have decided to try on the role of parent-coach, it's time to put what you've learned into practice. True, it's all well and good to read about having patience or to be reminded of using new skills, and quite another thing to put them to work in the real world. Don't worry; you've got what it takes. Perfection is not the goal in coaching teens. Connection is.

The qualities and skills you will need are learnable. Part Two of *Parent as Coach* will teach you *how* to integrate these techniques into your daily interaction with your teen. The foundation for the parent-coach relationship with your teen has been laid; now it is up to you to build on it together.

We all want positive relationships with our maturing children. As adults, we have the responsibility to take the first step, and to keep learning and applying to our daily parenting the important elements of coaching that I have described. We must commit to making a difference in young lives by committing to changing *ourselves*—so that we can learn to build lasting, respectful relationships with the next generation.

NOTES

★

PART TWO:
SEVEN WAYS TO COACH
YOUR TEEN

RESPECT

LISTEN

UNDERSTAND

APPRECIATE

SUPPORT

PROMOTE RESPONSIBILITY

NOURISH INDEPENDENCE

PART TWO:
SEVEN WAYS TO COACH YOUR TEEN

The <u>FIRST</u> Way to Coach Your Teen

"If you RESPECT me, I will hear you."

LEARNING RESPECT

If our desired outcome as parent-coaches is to forge loving relationships with our teens and help them prepare for the future, we must start by letting our children know that we value them as individuals and have faith in them. We show this by employing the Seven Ways—we endeavor to respect their humanity, hear them out, try to understand their viewpoints, appreciate their unique qualities, stand behind them, hold them responsible, and help them to become independent. It all begins with respect.

Webster defines the verb *respect* as "to treat with special consideration or high regard." Notice that the word *deserve* is left out of the definition. Respect is something that all people need and want just for being alive. We must treat teens with consideration simply because they are human beings who are doing their job—maturing into adults.

We can communicate respect to our teens in many different forms. Respect can come across in our words, body language, attentiveness, or in our ability to absorb the information young people share with us without jumping to conclusions or trying to solve their problems. Simply acting from a coaching perspective, with the focus on the teen, shows respect.

Two of my clients found ways to make respect tangible for themselves:

Tami

Tami, a single mother of twelve-year-old twins, confided in me that she could respect her son, Robert, a straight-A student, but found it difficult to respect her daughter, Leslie, because she was hard to manage, outspoken, and did not do well in school. Tami had established a precedent in her home that respect was attached to her children's performance and behavior. She found lots of ways to praise the "good" son and found herself mostly in conflict with the "bad" daughter. She inadvertently perpetuated the good/bad distinction by communicating respect only when Leslie or Robert did something that she deemed worthy of her praise and loving attention.

I asked Tami to consider showing equal respect for both of her children, *just for being individuals*. This was an eye-opener into her own behavior, and she was willing to give it a try. "But how?" she wondered.

We talked about simply using the word *respect* in conversation with both of her children, and how to stop using the actual regard for them as a reward or tool for praise. I asked Tami to think hard about both teens' wonderful qualities (as opposed to accomplishments), different in each child, and to respect them for simply possessing them. She promised to stop saying "respect" in relation to either teen's specific behavior, success, or failure, but to use it as a positive, unconditional expression of esteem.

"I started using the word *respect* in my day-to-day conversations with both my kids," she told me later. "My daughter, the more difficult one, just lapped it up. She really perked up when I told her that I respected her strength in making a difficult decision. Just using that word with her seemed to open her up. By using this word, I was able to put aside any judgments that I might have had about her behavior or the situation."

Tami mentioned that she now uses the word *respect* as a coaching tool. "It has become a kind of reminder, or 'trigger,' for me. When I think *respect*, I end up saying things that sound more supportive and encouraging than I have before. Both my kids know I respect them now, but it's my daughter who's had the greatest benefit. Her attitude has really improved, and she talks to me more than she ever has."

Jim

Jim, a divorced father whose teenage daughter, Trina, lives in another state, decided to incorporate the concept of *honor* into his thinking and speaking, as a way of showing respect. He tried to think of ways in which he could honor his daughter over the telephone.

He found casual ways to fit the word *honor* into conversations with Trina. He didn't attach its use to any kind of situation or problem, but rather used it to communicate the fact that he honored her for who she is. This resulted in making their long-distance relationship more intimate. Jim reported that this way of being with his daughter opened her up to trusting him more, even over the phone.

SHOWING RESPECT

Has anyone ever said "I respect you" to you? How did it feel? Acknowledging your respect for someone is an affirmation of their being. Teenagers are ravenous for this type of confirmation; it lets them know they're not alone, and that they're on the right track.

Examine your own personal definition of respect. Do you *show* respect for your teen? Other teens? Perhaps you respect your child in your heart, but are afraid or embarrassed to come out and say "I respect you" directly to him.

Your teen may not know you respect him until you actually say so. Telling other adults that you respect your kids does not create the same connection as telling them directly. Go ahead and ask your teenager, "How do you like to be respected?" Take note of his answers, and do not criticize, just listen. There! You've shown respect.

Practice #1: SAY IT

Try using the word respect in your vocabulary with your teenager—in a respectful tone! Try to say it consciously at least once daily over the next few weeks. At the end of each day, sit quietly and ask yourself how you used it today, and what the result was.

Practice #2: REHEARSAL

Each morning as you look in the mirror, take a full minute to say to yourself, "I respect you." Mean it. Get used to hearing yourself say the word respect. It will be easier to say and show to others if you can first learn to say it to yourself.

Practice #3: QUALITIES

Write a list of all the adults whom you respect, and why. Accomplishments aside, what particular qualities do you respect them for?

Now add to the list all of the teenagers you know. Write down the good qualities of each teenager on the list. Put the list in your pocket, wallet, or purse, and look at it daily for the next two weeks. Start using words that describe the qualities, not the actions, that you respect in your teen.

NOTES

The <u>SECOND</u> Way to Coach Your Teen

"If you LISTEN to me, I will feel understood."

LEARNING TO LISTEN

Listening is a skill, and ultimately an art. Have you ever trampled on someone's sentences, then thought, "I should try to be a better listener"? Here's your chance: *The number-one complaint I hear from teenagers is that no one listens to them.*

Webster defines the verb *listen* as "to make a conscious effort to hear; to attend to closely, so as to hear." Webster was obviously a teenager once! Teens need to feel listened to—and heard. Really heard.

To focus on and change your listening habits, start by listening with attentive ears. Listen to actively understand, not just to respond. Considerate listening is a voluntary action, not a passive reflex. You *can* gain control of your listening process. Revisit the basic skills of a good coach as you tune into the other person's point of view. Remember that the goal is to *listen to understand*. Practice on everyone you know, and incorporate these elements of listening well into your "silent" repertoire:

> **LISTEN** openly, before passing judgment;
> **LISTEN** for the other person's point of view;
> **LISTEN** for the "core" or underlying issue.

Consider listening as part of the circle of communication made up of speaking and listening. Taking part in completing the full circle is an act of respect toward a human being, your dialogue partner.

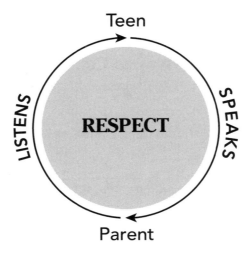

In this manner, listening becomes an integral, active expression of respect that accelerates into perpetual motion: Listening. Respect. More listening. More respect. The more our teenagers are being heard, the more they will confide in us and *say what is true for them*. This opens the way for a trusting and safe relationship.

Being a good listener is one way to communicate respect to your teenager, which you will in turn receive back from her. When your listening skills are needed, take a deep breath and remember your role as parent-coach. Keep the emphasis on your teen, and off of yourself.

Two of my clients found a way to listen and to focus on the speaker—their teenager—rather than on their own interpretations or reactions to what was being said:

Dan

Dan, a father and freelance writer, works with "point of view" every day. He realized that he could put this concept to use in listening to his daughter, Laura. "I now try to listen from *her* point of view, and try to remember what being sixteen felt like. Just being with her in that mode is refreshing because I can physically relax and not get so wound up about what *I* think. She just wants to share what her day was like, and doesn't need me to intervene, interrupt, or interpret. Being a parent-coach has made a big difference in the quality of our conversations. I talk less and listen more."

Robin

Robin, a single mom of three teens, reached the same conclusion: "In my work as a consultant, I have to listen carefully to my clients all the time. I never thought of listening to my *teenagers* that way until now. I'm not perfect at it, but I am more conscious of "keeping *me* out of their story" and letting their words be about them, not about my ideas. I have kind of a big personality and usually like to run the show, but that attitude does not work with my teenagers."

Robin discovered that listening well goes beyond improving communications. It can have healing properties. "I now have some new coaching tools, such as listening for the core issue that allows me to hear what is really going on," she says. "After our last conversation, my sixteen-year-old daughter, Kim, seemed to figure out for herself how to solve the problem she was having within five minutes of our talk—and I was just listening!"

SHOWING THAT WE'RE LISTENING

Think about the purposes that listening serves. We receive information, and process it in a thousand different ways into forms of understanding that are relevant to us. Now think about why we talk. We talk in order to impart information, sometimes to solicit an opinion or confirmation, sometimes not.

Have you ever called someone "just to talk"? Have you ever been talking with a friend about one thing and found yourself relating your entire busy schedule to her, even though it had nothing to do with that person? *You* were the one who needed to work out that information in your own mind. If you were lucky, your friend kept her mouth shut and let you ramble on, articulating the information so that you yourself could hear it and make sense of it. By listening to you, she allowed you to listen to yourself.

Consciously examine how you listen. When your teenager does open up, what are you listening for? Do you listen with the assumption that the speaker wants your advice, and prepare yourself to come up with a solution? Note your body language. Are you critical or judgmental in the way that you listen?

Teenagers can tell if you are really paying attention to them. Try listening with your full attention, and with *intention*.

Practice #1: POST IT
Write on a 3x5 card or sticky note: Listen to Understand. Look at it at least ten times a day for three days. Consciously take charge of your listening habits, and begin to put your "mantra" into practice. Don't give up on this! Continue to remind yourself over time by repeating, "Listen to understand." Keep track of the results.

Practice #2: ATTENTION
Just stop . . . the next time a teenager starts talking to you. Put down your book, stop reading the newspaper, stop doing the dishes. Take a breath, and switch gears. Turn to your son or daughter and offer your full, undivided attention while they are talking. Face them directly while you listen. Keep quiet and don't interrupt them; they may need to process their thoughts out loud a bit.

Practice #3: ACCESSIBILITY
Reserve one night a week and call it your Listening Night. Turn off the TV and put off all distractions—including answering the phone. Make yourself available to your teenager. Try something like, "I am one hundred percent available this evening to help you with your Spanish homework. When you're done, let's go get some ice

---

cream." Practice clearing a space in your schedule that is devoted solely to the relationship, and concentrate on listening first, not on fixing or solving a problem.

NOTES

★

The <u>THIRD</u> Way to Coach Your Teen

"If you UNDERSTAND me, I will feel appreciated."

LEARNING TO UNDERSTAND MORE DEEPLY

Does anyone reading this not wish to be understood? The desire to feel understood by our family, friends, coworkers—even the customer service agent on the end of a telephone line—is fundamental to us all.

Accept the notion that, like you, your teenager seeks to be understood. Consider the enormous changes and challenges that young people face every day. Teens not only want someone to respect and listen to them, they crave the end result of those actions. They crave compassionate understanding.

Webster defines the verb *understand* as "to know or grasp the meaning, importance, intention, or motive of; to perceive or discern the meaning of." Seek to know the meaning, importance, intention, or motive of the son or daughter whom you love so much. Find out where they're coming from. Keep the cycle of respect and listening between you and your teen going, and build on that with a response that allows the young person to feel understood.

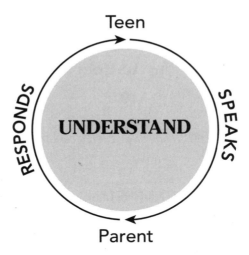

Who wants to hear that old saw, "When I was your age . . ."? Two of my clients found the ability to reach an understanding based on personal experience or knowledge, *but to keep that information in the background* and to focus on their teen:

Manuel

Manuel is a devoted parent of a daughter, eleven, and a son, thirteen. With them, Manuel started to apply understanding as a goal in his listening technique, resisting the urge to relate his insight to his own past experience. In one situation with his son, George, he recalled, "After a long conversation with my son about grades and some of his problem areas, I said to him, 'I think I understand what you are going through. It must be tough to be in a class of thirty students and be able to stay on task.' I used the word *understand* directly—and I really did feel as though I understood, because I have been there myself. I just never told him that before. He appreciated my concern and understanding, and seemed more relaxed after our talk."

Joelle

Joelle relied on finding a new perspective to help her understand her daughter better. "My daughter, Linda, has ADD [attention deficit disorder] and is very disorganized in keeping track of schedules and getting homework in on time. I decided to read up on ADD to learn more about it. I now have a better understanding of how her mind works and why she needs additional help with her schedule. I tell her I understand her better now. I am more available to help her now. Before, I would be frustrated and tell her so—and that would make everything worse. Coming from a place of understanding about what *she* is going through has helped me tremendously."

SHOWING THAT WE UNDERSTAND

Did you feel understood by adults as a teen? If so, try to recall what made you feel that way. If not, consider breaking that cycle, and begin to hand out some understanding and compassion to young people. Share their perspectives, without any other obligation. Understanding is achieved through empathy and concern; it doesn't come from having all the answers.

Make a sincere attempt to understand where your teen is coming from. Instead of dwelling on the vast social changes between your youth and hers, focus on commonalities. While governments may topple and time marches on, human nature remains the same.

Practice #1: FIND OUT

Ask your teen if she feels that you understand her or if she feels heard. You can do this in a general sense or relate it to a specific situation. During conversation, find the right time to ask, "Do you think I understand you?" Remember to listen when your teen responds, and don't be defensive if the answer isn't to your liking. Accept her answer and use her insights to further your understanding next time. Understanding is not a one-time event—the light bulb doesn't always go on and stay on. You can check in with your teen often about this.

Practice #2: SAY IT

Start using the term "I understand" with your teenager—
but be careful not to overdo it. Using this language with
teenagers reinforces our desire to understand. Before
you say the words, put yourself in their shoes and imagine how life must be for young people today. Try saying
the word understand as it actually happens with your
teen at least once a day for the next three weeks. By
vocalizing the expression, you may find that you understand him more than you thought you did.

Practice #3: BREATHE

Break the habit of offering advice or problem solving
in favor of understanding. When your teenager talks to
you, prepare yourself to listen to understand by taking
two deep breaths before speaking. This will slow you
down and give you time to alter, or at least delay, your
usual reaction. As you breathe, remind yourself to seek to
understand and not jump to conclusions.

Of course, conversations arise quickly. If you need help
remembering to breathe and focus, buy some colored
adhesive dots from an office supply store. Stick one on
your watch, or in your calendar, or on the refrigerator.
When you see the dots, let them prompt you to breathe
and shift your focus to one of understanding, rather than
reflex, before you speak to your teen.

NOTES

The <u>FOURTH</u> Way to Coach Your Teen

"If you APPRECIATE me, I will know your support."

LEARNING APPRECIATION

Admiration, praise, thanks—all are expressions of appreciation of a human being's qualities and talents. Teenagers have reported to me that receiving praise in the way of sincere appreciation for something they have done, even if the task is small and the tribute fleeting, is something that they remember and that makes them feel good. We're not talking about the out-of-proportion applause for a first-grader's finger painting; with teenagers, showing appreciation is not that simple. We must not only sound sincere in our admiration, we must be sincere, or teens will call us on it for being phony.

Of course, showing appreciation to the first-grader was fairly easy; she ate it up and gave you instant feedback with smiles, hugs, and a happy attitude. With teenagers, it's more subtle. While they may project otherwise, teens don't want us to hold back or be aloof. They want us to continue giving them our praise and admiration. However, they want these things from us in a new way that honors who they are at this stage in life.

Appreciate is defined as "to be conscious of the significance, desirability, or worth of." Think about how you appreciate a co-worker or neighbor, and how you express that appreciation. Use that as your standard for giving appreciation to teens. They need to be treated as adults in this instance, not as children. They also want attention or compliments without strings attached, not as bait for something you want done or as evidence of what a good parent you are.

A parent-coach gives appreciation freely and authentically. We reinforce respect, listening, and understanding by showing appreciation. My clients Barbara and Randall discovered how the simplest recognition plays a part in making a teen feel part of the family structure, and ultimately part of society:

Barbara

Barbara is a forty-one-year-old mother of a twelve-year-old daughter, Stacy. As a child and as an adult, Barbara felt a lack of appreciation from her parents, and as a result, stored up resentment toward them that she had to work out. After her parents passed away, their friends mentioned to Barbara that her parents had said how much they'd appreciated her care when they were sick. "I was struck by this," Barbara recalls, "because they had never told me that they appreciated me directly. I was moved by this disparity, and have vowed to tell my daughter how much she means to me and how much I appreciate her good qualities."

Barbara now makes a point of speaking her thoughts of appreciation to Stacy, as opposed to only telling her friends. "When I tell her I appreciate something that she does, even if it is something simple like, 'I appreciate you doing the dishes tonight,' she beams and gives me back a sincere 'Thanks!' She has even started to tell me that she appreciates the things I do for her!"

Randall

Randall, a fifty-year-old father, discovered how the power of appreciation "includes" a teenager and reinforces his good deeds. He asked his fifteen-year-old son how he likes to be appreciated. Randall said, "After he looked at me like I was from the moon, he realized I was serious and said, 'I like to be acknowledged for what I do. I don't like it when you go overboard and *say good job, good job* all the time like I'm a little kid, though. When it comes to appreciation, I like to be thanked for doing the stuff that I do, like taking out the garbage, but not in a big way. I just like to be recognized.'"

SHOWING APPRECIATION

The next time you catch yourself telling a friend or family member how great your kids are, make a mental note to track them down and tell them the same. Showing appreciation does double duty; it provides evidence of your esteem and demonstrates polite manners—something you would naturally do in thanking a waiter for more ice water. We sometimes forget to treat our loved ones as well as we do strangers.

Don't take teenagers' efforts for granted. Acknowledge their contributions to your household and to your life, and you may find this attitude reciprocated, as Barbara did with her daughter.

Practice #1: INVENTORY

Write down the ways that you like to receive appreciation, and the things that you like to be appreciated for. Consider external appreciation as a commodity that you want, and decipher how you get it and from whom. Next, look at that model through a teenager's eyes. In that frame of mind, write a list of the ways you might show appreciation for your teenager. Keep the list handy, such as in a daily calendar, and look at it once a day for three weeks. Assess which of those ways worked best with your son or daughter.

Practice #2: SAY IT

Incorporate the word appreciate into your vocabulary when directly speaking with your teen: "I appreciate the way you..." Fill in the blank. This will be a lifelong practice.

Practice #3: PERSPECTIVE

Where does your appreciation come from? Learning to value others for their unique contributions to the world means suspending your personal judgments about them. Begin to train your thoughts by using a simple phrase in your mind: Say "I cherish you" silently, in regard to your teen, each time you come into his or her presence. Let this fundamental thought determine how you send out your love and appreciation.

NOTES

★

The <u>FIFTH</u> Way to Coach Your Teen

"If you SUPPORT me as I try new things, I will become responsible."

LEARNING HOW AND WHEN TO SUPPORT

Support comes in many varieties—emotional, intellectual, physical, financial, spiritual. The type and level of support that teens need changes over the years. One minute they may accept and appreciate our emotional support, and the next day they may want little or no emotional connection to us at all. They have reached a period in their development when a separation or emancipation from their parents naturally begins to occur.

This is not the time to dig in your heels and buck the tide. Remember to remain fluid and open as a parent-coach, and to be attentive to the sometimes daily rise and fall of your teen's need for—or ambivalence to—different kinds of support. This is a good time to recall that your primary role as administrator is a thing of the past.

As parents, we may instinctually support our children in the manner that we received help when we were young. If our parents gave us a money allowance, we give an allowance. If they required us to work for it, we ask the same of our kids. Those of us whose parents were very engaged in emotional or moral support tend toward replicating that. However, some people who received little or no praise as children will heap it on their children, overcompensating.

When to support your teen is equally as important as the method of encouragement you choose. The dual delivery system of *how* and *when* support is provided plays an important role in fostering future responsibility and independence, as we shall see in the following pages. Recall that a good coach sets and lives up to standards. You can achieve a balance between giving too much and giving too little by knowing your own boundaries, or how much you can give while remaining true to yourself—and by placing the emphasis on your teen's growth, determining whether the support in question will enhance your teen's experience in the world.

Two of my clients learned to adapt to their teens' changing situations and found new ways in which to support them:

Betsy

Betsy has a grandson named Ben whom she parents full time. During his freshman year in high school, his grades began to drop. Betsy reacted instinctively, nagging Ben about unfinished homework and criticizing him for his indifference toward school. After switching to the parent-coach mode, she instead began to see her grandson as an individual with a crisis.

As his grades slid further, the two finally consulted with the school counselor, who suggested some options that might help. Moving to a smaller school with a different style of teaching appealed to Ben, and Betsy decided that she could support him financially at a smaller school if he did the research and filled out the applications.

Eager to find some level of success, he did everything she asked and switched to a new school, where his grades improved dramatically. In focusing on support and not judgment, Betsy found new ways to encourage her grandson in his academic life.

Loretta

Loretta is a stay-at-home mom with two teenagers and two small children. Her oldest, an artistically talented eighteen-year-old named John, was struggling with after–high school plans. He was not in school, lived at home, worked full time, and partied almost every night until late with his friends.

Loretta and her husband could not decide how to support their son during this time. They alternated between wanting to throw him out, versus keeping the calm by not saying anything and waiting for the situation to change on its own.

Trying out a coaching approach, Loretta decided to be direct and ask John to tell her what kind of support he needed at this time in his life. She initiated an open-ended discussion about support from *his* point of view, promising to listen to whatever he said and not judge him for it. It took Loretta five attempts to break the ice, but eventually what John had bottled up for years came pouring out.

He indicated that his parents' unrelenting pressure to go to college was in effect paralyzing him to do anything else. This conversation set the stage for ongoing communication between them, and they crafted a plan of support together that worked for all concerned. They discussed an apprenticeship program for furniture making that seemed more in line with John's interests. The program was so successful for him that he decided on his own to enroll in some community college classes geared toward becoming a specialty carpenter.

One conversation opened up so much. Loretta and her husband had to make the shift from administrator to coach in their role as parents in order to save the relationship with their oldest son.

SHOWING SUPPORT

One dictionary definition of *support* is "to further the interests or cause of." This is especially so with a growing human being. Show that you care about your teen's future by supporting the interests that add to her life experience and that nurture her potential. Parental support must hinge on teens' current needs—to mature into their own persons—not on what seemed best yesterday. Respectful support should be given on an individual basis, not dictated by convention or a set timetable, or by the desire for our children to succeed at a particular thing. Teenagers need to feel supported in their own right.

If you have more than one child, compare notes. Is the support you give them based on who they are as individuals, rather than on how you were parented or on gender stereotypes? Do you provide physical, emotional, spiritual, intellectual, *and* financial support, and is it wanted or needed? Or are you short-changing anyone in one or more of these areas?

Again, remember to stay flexible as a coach. Your teen is not you. Assess the unique qualities of your son or daughter, and think about finding meaningful ways to support them: Your presence at a swim meet might mean more to your son than helping him through a loss after the fact. Or, financially supporting a stay at an astrology camp might be a more concrete show of faith than telling your daughter she can do whatever she sets her mind to.

Build on the previous skills involving respect, listening, understanding, and appreciation to get in tune with what kind of—and how much—support your teenager needs.

Practice #1: IMPROVE

Take written inventory of what kind of financial, emotional, physical, intellectual, and spiritual support you offer your teenager. Note which area you support your teen in the least. Think about your teenager in light of that need, then create one way in which you can give added support to your child. Practice this as a routine, and you will add depth to your support repertoire. Or find an expert on the subject who can provide guidance in one of those areas, and make the connection for your teen.

Practice #2: TRADITION

Create a tradition of periodic outings with your teenager, without other adults or brothers and sisters along if possible. Make it a routine your teen can depend on. Go out for pizza together on a certain night of the week. Or let him choose the agenda for a trip downtown or to the beach. Remember that quantity time at this age sets the stage for regular communication. All you have to do is to be there and engage—leave that cell phone or sports page at home!

Practice #3: SAY IT

Show your teenager that you are there for her by including the word support in your conversations. You don't have to guess about her needs. Ask your daughter directly, "What kind of support do you feel you need from me/us?" Open up the lines of communication around this subject, and include it in your language from now on. Refrain from being critical or defensive when your teen says what she needs; you may be surprised at what she has to say, so listen well.

NOTES

★

The <u>SIXTH</u> Way to Coach Your Teen

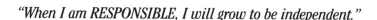

"When I am RESPONSIBLE, I will grow to be independent."

LEARNING TO PROMOTE RESPONSIBILITY

You have two choices as a parent: You can follow your growing children through life cleaning up after their mistakes, or you can give them the tools to do so themselves. Being a parent-coach requires that you accept that your children will eventually be managing life on their own. When you have listened to them with respect and understanding, and when you have shown them support and appreciation, they will be ready (and obligated!) to accept increasing responsibility.

To be responsible, by definition, is to be "trustworthy," a virtue that assumes two parties, a giver and a receiver of trust. The other half of the coaching relationship—the receiver's end—does not just *take* continually. The goal in coaching is to provide the tools for the athlete or businessperson or teenager to give more of themselves. This does not mean we automatically cut them loose when they are "ready"; as coaches, we must design safe steps, or *passages*, that will assist them with the transition.

How you do this will depend greatly on your family's lifestyle, your individual style of parenting, and your teen's level of maturity. Helping your child take on responsibility is a personal task, and one that requires a fluid approach. Be prepared for more trial and error in this area than in exploring the previous nurturing skills.

Don't look at isolated "failures" as incompetence or fruitless efforts on both your parts. Promoting responsibility is the act of proposing a challenge to your teen: *Can you do this? Will you do this? How well?* We discover our boundaries and potential by both failing and succeeding at life's challenges. And, often, an unsuccessful endeavor establishes a wish to try harder next time.

So, start small, and don't tie your teen's performance to instant gratification. Let assuming responsibility lead to more long-term benefits: less parent-teen friction over chores, greater freedom to drive or travel—even the assumption of responsibility on your part for something that your teen would like from you on a regular basis. Taking on responsibility has to do with changing roles and routines, and you'll have to decide for yourself where to make nips and tucks in the family schedule.

My clients Tim and Sam were able to do just that:

Tim

Tim is the father of two stepchildren, Jamal and Vera, both in their teens. His wife is gone in the mornings to work by the time the kids get up. So Tim took on the responsibility for waking the two of them each morning to get ready for school. This routine always met with great resistance, especially from one of the teenagers, who is *not* a morning person.

After years of battles about getting up in the morning, Tim decided to buy both his children alarm clocks and to let them get themselves up; then he would take them to school. This was a risky enterprise, because Tim knew that they might not get up, and they might miss school. After considering promoting responsibility this way, he gave it a try by first introducing the idea to the kids, and then making agreements with them regarding their responsibility and his part of the deal, taking them to school.

After some trial and error, the two teens eventually learned to get themselves up and ready for school. They started to become accountable to each other, and more importantly, to themselves, to get going in the morning. Tim reported that creating the *opportunity* for his son and daughter to accept some responsibility showed him their potential, and set the stage for further progress. He started giving them additional responsibilities, and enjoyed finding new ways to help them in becoming adept at self-management.

Sam

Sam, a divorced father of two teenagers—Caitlin, thirteen, and Melanie, fifteen—had issues about cleanliness and chores being done. After years of battling his daughters about putting their dirty laundry in the wash area and putting clean clothes away, he decided to take another tack. He first clarified for *himself* what his expectations were around laundry. Sam learned that his expectations were different from those of his ex-wife, with whom his daughters lived half the time.

After he was clear in his expectations, he discussed his thoughts with Caitlin and Melanie. Together they agreed on a plan for which day of the week each of them—Dad included—would do their own laundry, including washing, drying, folding, and ironing. Sam not only gave his daughters a responsibility with clear guidelines, he gave them a *sense* of responsibility in valuing their contribution to the household. The laundry became a non-issue, freeing Sam up to spend time with his daughters in other ways.

SHOWING RESPONSIBLE BEHAVIOR

Accepting responsibility is a big step for teens. Again, we cannot ask them to do it "cold turkey"—this is an area where they need real, live guidance to give them the confidence and the ability to go ahead and follow through with it. We must model this behavior for them by being responsible ourselves.

Let your teen see you taking responsibility for your finances, your possessions, your commitments. And admit your mistakes when they happen. Try something like, "I made the best decision for good reasons at the time, but now I see it was a mistake." Your teen will feel free to enter into conversations with you about how he can handle responsibilities.

When you decide on an area of responsibility to work on, define your expectations, and then clarify in your mind exactly what you will ask of your teenager. Look ahead to how he can meet your request, staying open and working out some possibilities; often there is more than one "right" way. Finally, make your request, demonstrating specifically what you want done. The simple act of showing eliminates much of the fear and ambiguity of taking on a new responsibility.

For instance, if you entrust your son with weekly cleaning of the bathroom, simply assigning the task or promising to check up is not enough. How does one clean a bathroom? If you've been doing it for years, you already know. Point out the target spots— toilet, tub, sink, mirrors, floor. Toilet and tub may be obvious, but *floor*? Perhaps your son hadn't thought of that one. Go through the motions, then let him show you how it's done. You can't just complain after the fact when the room is not clean; you must be thorough in your explanation and demonstration of what needs doing. This cuts down on excuses *and* unmet responsibilities.

Teach your teen responsibility in this way: Start small with household chores. Show your son how you balance your checkbook or change the oil in your car; then let him try it. By getting him started in this way, you'll create *momentum*, something we all like to ease us into a task, and you'll foster a sense of responsibility in showing him how he fits into collective society. In other words, you are saying to your teen: *"These are things we all must do; here's how. Become one of us."*

Practice #1: AGREEMENTS

Practice designing and making clear requests of your teen, and ask for her accountability by making agreements. Don't assume that she knows what you want or how much responsibility you want her to shoulder. Be clear in your communication, and let your teen know that she has an obligation as someone who will soon be an adult to try her best to fulfill your request.

Try something like, "I have a request of you. From now on can you manage to keep your dirty laundry in the basket, not all over the laundry room? Can we agree on this?" Be prepared to negotiate, and know where you stand with your expectations. Know what your bottom line is, and you can be flexible about how things get done.

Practice #2: BUDGETS

Some teenagers think that the money fountain flows endlessly. Create budgets for expenses. Make a list of your and your teen's expenditures for a week or a month. Show him how those expenses come out of the monthly budget. This takes some of the mystery out of where the money comes from and gives him a dose of reality on how small expenses add up quickly.

Create a chart of accounts for your annual income and expenses. Ask your teenager to take on partial management of the budget. (After being consistent with this, I am happy to say that each time we go clothes shopping, my son asks me, "Mom, what is our budget for this today?")

Practice #3: SAY IT

Practice saying the word responsible in communicating with your teen when you really are requesting that she be responsible. Watch your language to see if you are expecting responsibility before clearly requesting it. Go ahead and use the word in making pacts with your teen. Instead of "You can't use the car on weekends unless you promise to clean it," try something like "From now on, would you like to take on the responsibility for keeping the car clean in exchange for being able to use it on Friday nights?"

NOTES

★

The **SEVENTH** Way to Coach Your Teen

"In my INDEPENDENCE, I will respect you and love you all of my life."

LEARNING TO NOURISH INDEPENDENCE

Personal independence is about having a sense of self that allows one to strike out confidently into the world. It is no accident that Webster's definition of *independent* includes "self-directed, self-maintained, self-governing." Fostering this sense of the power of self, or autonomy, in your teenager happens when you step back and let him handle things in his own style (for by now you have a pretty good idea of what that style is!). Your teenager has shown a level of maturity that becomes collateral in your mind for risking the consequences of his choices. You have built upon all of the previous skills to engender a responsible attitude in him, and now you can risk his first flights of independence.

Nourishing your child's eventual independence from you takes the most fortitude and finesse of all the parent-coach tasks. It is a matter of striking a balance, encouraging your teen to be self-sufficient while retaining a healthy interdependence and connection with you and others. "Self-directed" does not mean self-absorbed. We must leave our teens with the ability to manage themselves in terms of behavior, choices, and commitments, and at the same time be able to give *of* themselves and contribute to their families, communities, and to the larger world. The independence that teenagers crave is as much a need to become self-determining and accountable within society as it is about separation from you, the adult.

At this time, examine your mixed feelings about letting your children go. Sometimes it seems as though they'll always be your babies; other times, you feel as though their independence from you can't arrive quickly enough! Accept that the reality is somewhere in between, and that it is natural for teenaged humans to want to become autonomous and capable, and to develop in this direction. Continue your day-to-day habits as parent-coach: speaking with respect, listening to understand, appreciating and supporting your teens' gifts and pursuits, and promoting responsibility.

Two of my clients relate how using the combined parent-coach skills resulted in truly independent behavior by their teens:

Sophie

Sophie is a divorced mom of one very smart, but disorganized fourteen-year-old daughter, Angie. Sophie's ex-husband decided to treat Angie's problem by buying her a large, notebook-sized day planner, like the one he uses in his law practice. He tried to teach her to use it, but she found the large task of scheduling and time management to be too much.

"After many tormented months," Sophie relates, "I asked my daughter to describe her frustration with the day planner." The young woman confided that she felt pressured to be as responsible as her father, and that she was overwhelmed by the complicated planner. After discussing the matter with her ex-husband, Sophie bought her daughter a small, simple planner that she immediately liked.

"Instead of having her father or me manage her appointments," Sophie says, "she now carries the small planner around and feels a new sense of responsibility as it relates to her schedule. She had the wrong method (for her) for being organized."

By giving Angie the right tool for accepting responsibility, Sophie allowed her daughter to think and act more independently with her schedule.

Jack

Jack finds the parent-coach relationship to be an ideal stepping stone to independence for his son, Rory, a high-school senior. "When I use the parent-coach approach with my son, I think about my days as a basketball player in high school. My coach would get me to perform my best by encouraging me to think when out on the court. He taught me to use my judgment in the critical moments of each play."

Rory had to make a difficult decision about college. His buddies planned to attend a local community college, while Rory was interested in a unique program at a university across the country. Jack taught his son to consider the pros and cons of each route, and in the end Rory discovered a third option that worked for him: go to a university offering a similar program only fifty miles away, and stay in touch with his friends on the weekends.

"I am trying to be that kind of coach with my son, in life as well as sports," Jack says. "I remind him that he is on the 'court' of life's challenges, and that I am here on the sidelines as an advocate and a guide. I can't make his decisions for him, but I can be here in a consistent way. I think he appreciates the coach-type approach."

SHOWING THEM THE WAY TO INDEPENDENCE

If you are hanging onto your teen's childhood by doing everything for her, let go of some of your control. Accept the fact that your lovely, little girl will someday manage life on her own. *Prepare her for life*—how to shop for groceries, how to cook, do laundry, manage finances, use a map, use public transportation, make independent decisions using good judgment.

Or, if you believe that independence means being "on your own" to do as you please, *set some boundaries*. Although your teen is becoming an adult, in the future she will still have to operate within certain limits—financially, socially, schedule-wise. None of us can really just do whatever we want whenever we want to. Being free within specified parameters, such as making an agreement that she may drive your car as long as she pays for gas or that she may spend Saturday as she pleases if she is home by a certain time, teaches your teen the kind of independence tempered by responsibility that she can expect in college, on the job, or even in an informal social situation like a backyard barbecue.

Besides preparing and guiding your teenager toward independence, you must acknowledge her changing stature. Respect her privacy, and give her some decompression time when she needs it; with studies, jobs, and extracurricular activities, your teen is not on your schedule anymore! Search for the balance that will affirm her as an almost-adult, while holding her to the rules of home and school. With a little coaching, most teenagers come to realize that they can become their own persons with a certain amount of independence, and yet preserve their ties with family members and the rest of the community around them.

Practice #1: OPPORTUNITIES

Independence is attained incrementally as your teen feels a sense of responsibility and ownership for something material or emotional. Be on the lookout for opportunities to turn responsibility into independent action. For instance, your son has taken a serious interest in his appearance. Besides using the all-important hair gel, he chooses clothes and actually irons shirts and cleans his shoes. He has shown that he can stay within a budget on shopping trips. Now is the time to stop asking him about his laundry, to let him be responsible for buying all of his wardrobe (including socks and underwear!), and to compliment his appearance and let him know he is doing a good job.

Practice #2: RETREAT

Let your teenager pass through quiet or lethargic or tense mood changes. Try not to think of her behavior as brooding or mopey. Be okay in the silence. Wait. This is a teen's internal processing time, and you should encourage it, not resist it.

When your teenager comes home from school, give her a "nonalcoholic happy hour." Take the pressure off the time between school and home by allowing her to unwind before dinner, chores, homework, or evening activities. Provide a snack perhaps, and let her decide whether to enjoy it solo or in company. Even if a time-out of just ten or fifteen minutes is offered, your teen will know that you respect her need for some time on her own.

Practice #3: CHOICE

Say the words "What do you choose?" or "What will your choice be?" when supporting your teen to make decisions for himself. One example is lawn mowing. If you are looking for a responsible choice from your teen, instead of nagging him to get on with the lawn, gently remind him of his agreement and let him decide how to fulfill it: "Since the lawn is your responsibility, will you be mowing it today or tomorrow? What will your choice be?" Wait for him to choose; don't force your answer on him.

Start this exercise in the early teen years. After a while, your teen will start saying on his own, "I choose . . ." or "My choice is . . ." One of the most lasting gifts a parent-coach can give young people is encouragement in making small decisions. This prepares them for the big judgments they'll have to make when you're not around.

NOTES

PART THREE:
COACHING QUESTIONS
PARENTS ASK

PART THREE:
COACHING QUESTIONS PARENTS ASK

I have preteens, nine and eleven. What can I do with parent-coach techniques now?

Begin to lay a foundation of respect and understanding now. Start practicing in small steps and gradually warm up to the role of coach. Though you are still a "parent-administrator," by absorbing coaching skills now you will be ready to adjust to the coming changes in your children as they happen.

This is also a good time to start a support group with other parents. You'll find comfort and solidarity in knowing that others share your concerns. Use this book to prompt discussion with other parents of preteens about how the coaching role can help parents adapt to children's transitional years.

I am tired, overwhelmed, frustrated, and distraught with my kids. Is it me, or is it the "teenager" in them? Where did all the joy, the hugs, the love go?

Parenting teenagers starts with managing *yourself*. Respect your own individuality. Learn to separate what is your "stuff" from what is their "stuff." If you are tired and overwhelmed, take care of these issues first. How can you listen to your own inner voice or the voices of those you love if your life is full of static? This may be the time to slow down your activities, cut yourself some slack, and give yourself room to examine where you are coming from as a parent.

Try placing a note card by your bed that says, "I will take care of myself today." Let that be the first thing you look at in the morning; *say it, and do it.* Do one thing that nourishes you, so that you will have the courage and the stamina and the patience to be the parent you want to be that day. Try this for one week, then notice how this practice carries over into your daily life.

I want my son to achieve what I didn't. Why don't you say much about achievement? What about success? How can I get my son to be successful?

Success and failure are words the parent-coach should reserve for goals and accomplishments, not to gauge a person's inner life or their way of being in the world. Please don't confuse the desire you have for your son to be successful with your profound love and respect for him, no matter what he does with his life, providing it is within legal and moral boundaries. Success and failure are not the true measure of a human being's worthiness of love and respect.

Accept the fact that your son may not live up to your expectations, or that he may follow his own path to even greater reward than you can imagine. What you *can* do is to help him learn to follow his heart. Tell him you love and respect him for who he is, and promise to support his decisions, even if they stray from your own values. If you nourish his independent and creative spirit, he may indeed reach greater heights than the vision you now hold for him.

My teenage son has low self-esteem. Do you have any tips?

Tell your son directly that you respect him in everyday conversation, without tying it to a particular action or accomplishment. Let him know that you respect him as a human being, plain and simple. Reinforcing this basic affirmation may help him internalize the thought as well.

Create an opportunity for success by helping him engage in something he's interested in, such as showing him how to redesign and paint his bedroom and asking him to finish it, or asking him to play the piano for a dinner party. Let him exercise his talents and find new ones. Feeling competent and responsible adds to self-esteem.

I'm a stepdad; I married a divorced woman with two teenage children. I seem to get no respect from the teens. What can I do to get their respect?

Turn the story around and think of ways that you can respect your stepchildren first. After all, they have endured the hardship of their parents' divorce, and they are trying to sort out not only who they are during this time, but who you are to them. Stop thinking that you deserve their respect, and stop making demands that they give it to you.

Instead, teach by example. Go easy, start small. Take it a day at a time, and focus on ways to let your stepchildren know how much you respect and appreciate them. Learn to separate the behavior from the *person*, and find a way to respect them for themselves. Start giving of yourself in such a way that shows your deep love and respect for the teens' mother, and your commitment to the family. This will get their attention.

My daughter lives with her mother two thousand miles away. I only talk to her on the phone and see her once a year. Does Parent as Coach work over the phone?

Yes, the parent-coach approach can work over the telephone. Teenagers are astute and can hear your meaning in your voice. As you listen on your end, keep the focus on your teen, and *listen to understand*, not just to respond to the two-way conversation.

Evaluate how often you call your daughter, and why. Do you only call to discuss the "big stuff"? That can be a turn-off. If you talk about (and listen to!) everyday matters, it will be easier to communicate about larger issues. And don't be disappointed or angry when your teen doesn't think to call; just pick up the slack and take responsibility for staying connected. If you are afraid to use words that express your deep love for her, muster your courage and *say what is so for you, and tell the truth.*

I have two teenage daughters. One is a straight-A student and a model young woman. The other has ADD and struggles in school and in life. I have trouble parenting two entirely different personalities. Any Parent as Coach ideas?

Forget the one-size-fits-all idea of parenting. Create clear expectations for both of your teenagers as individuals. Learn which guidelines work for both of them, as in family rules, and which chores or exceptions need to be customized to each one. Ask them both for their perspectives on things, and be ready to acknowledge each one's unique viewpoint.

Then, show your respect for this uniqueness by expressing admiration or appreciation to each of them separately. This will keep you from comparing one child with the other and will remind you of their distinct gifts. Learn to see the one who struggles as a treasure to your family; she may teach you things about life that you may not be able to see yourself.

My teenage son grunts a lot and doesn't give me any information about what's going on at school. Our conversations are all uncomfortable. Any ideas on how to open him up?

It's time to stop *trying* to open your son up and learn to make the space for him to open up on his own. Check out your listening and speaking skills. Are you too forceful? Does he think you are prying into his life? Try instead to understand where he is coming from: Does he have an overriding insecurity or anxiety about a relationship or grades? Is he a naturally shy person? Is he hurting in any way?

As a matter of course, let your teen know what is going on with you in a real and natural way. Let him in on some of *your* inner struggles and challenges, so he doesn't feel that he is the only one who has issues. When he doesn't want to chat, accept his intro-spective moods and give him some "think time." Even if it looks more like "space-out time," subconscious work goes on while he is resting from life's daily pressures.

My fifteen-year-old daughter has really changed in the past year. She is moody, aloof, and now runs with a bad crowd. How can the parent-coach approach help me with her?

Step back from these overwhelming changes, and center yourself first. Start by embracing the belief that all people, including your daughter, are essentially kind, gentle, and good, and that they are seeking a return to this state in their day-to-day lives. Being caught up in a "bad crowd" is your daughter's way of looking for her place of belonging and finding her sense of purpose in life—though she may not be aware of it at this time. When you are ready to talk to her, look past her temporary behaviors and actively respect her for who she is. Tell her so.

Encourage your teenager's search for her true nature by con-tinuing to separate your feelings about who she is versus what she does, and let her know that you see the two as separate. Should professional help seem appropriate, ask for support from counselors, therapists, or trained coaches for either of you, or both of you together. You may want to start by discussing some options with a high school counselor.

My son is defensive, so I am defensive back. It seems like all we do is fight and yell at each other. What can I do?

Take yourself out of "adversary" mode and switch to parent-coach mode. When your son is speaking (or yelling), are you bracing for battle and preparing to retaliate? Stop that posture. The proper response here is to step back and listen. When you're in the heat of the moment, STOP and take a breath or two to collect yourself. Try to get some perspective on what's really going on with your teenager underneath the outpouring of emotion.

Your task is not to try to manipulate your son into another state of being. The point here is to remind yourself that, as coach, you must set an example of behavior. Examine your motives for being defensive; after all, your son may have learned how to fight from you. Consider taking an anger-management class; ask for referrals from a therapist in your area. Focus on your own actions, then let them go, and let your teen take center stage as you model good listening behavior.

I'm trying the parent-coach approach, but my spouse is stubborn and won't listen to my explanations about this new stuff. Can I go it alone on this?

Yes, you can be a solo parent-coach. Lead by example. Try using some of the Seven Ways ideas with your spouse first, such as "listening to understand," as a way of testing out some of the practices in this book. When your mate notices a change in the atmosphere, point out how *Parent as Coach* helped you get there. In addition, try relating to your teenager on a one-to-one basis without other family members present, so your teen knows that you can be counted on to listen attentively and without passing judgment.

Remember, we become parent-coaches by learning to understand ourselves first. Examine your motives and the way in which you relate to people. Then commit to creating a more open and loving relationship with your teenager. Journal your observations.

I am a good parent and have been involved with my children throughout their lives. Are you blaming me for their mistakes? I already blame myself. I have done my best and they are still screwed up.

No blame. *Parent as Coach* invites you to look forward, not back. Renew or rebuild your relationship by trying out some of the suggestions in this book. Look inside your heart and imagine new ways to think about yourself and your teens; see if you can come from a place of understanding and put aside the "screwed up" line while you try out some new possibilities.

Every teenager needs support and kindness—even those who have made mistakes. Feeling guilty or heaping guilt on others won't serve anybody well. Revisit your commitment to parenting, and use it to adopt the parent-coach approach. Love is magic and can help you move past any notion of blame.

My thirteen-year-old daughter has multiple learning disabilities. She was a wild child, but now as a teen!—I am going crazy trying to manage her. What can I do?

Whatever you do, don't retreat in surrender. Learning or developmental disabilities require specialized attention from parents, professionals, schools, friends, and family members. If you know that your teenager has any diagnosed condition, be it physical, mental, or emotional, consult with professionals who can recommend appropriate treatment. Read books and check out Web sites, join a parent support group. Learn more, and keep on learning.

As a parent-coach, realize that your teenager needs your respect and understanding even more than most. Focus on ways you can praise and admire her. Spend as much time acknowledging her good traits as you do dwelling on the ones that drive you crazy. Tell your teenager you respect her, and that you understand how hard life must be for her sometimes.

What about drugs, violence, gangs, teen sex, AIDS, homelessness, and all the other "bad" things in the world that teens today are susceptible to? Why don't you address these things?

I acknowledge that our world is filled with problems, conflict, aggressions, and despair in the lives of youth everywhere. *Parent as Coach* offers an individual response to these concerns from the standpoint that some of the strife in modern society can be abated through the adoption of respectful and understanding relationships between adults and young people. The parent-coach approach involves the singular relationship between one adult and one teenager. That inspired teenager, in turn, can make a world of difference in another young life, in the community, and possibly in humankind in general.

Many community youth programs exist that address the urgent issues you mention. If necessary, take that step and get connected and involved with them. At the same time, don't deny the power of your own influence. The challenge raised in this book is, What are *you* going to do about the "teen" question? What kind of parent or adult will you be? Will you tear down or build up? Make a commitment to "volunteer" right in your own home, in your own family. One person can make a difference.

What about kids who are really on the edge—gang members, runaways, violent teenagers? Does Parent as Coach work for these young people, too?

Parent as Coach is not intended as crisis intervention, rather as a tool kit for building a new foundation. Still, the ideas in this book can be applied in almost any situation. Every teenager, no matter his or her predicament, needs compassion and understanding. Though it is sometimes too late for the *parent* to effectively intervene with a troubled teen (the family situation may be part of the original problem), *any adult* may use the parent-coach approach. Counselors in youth, church, or sports programs, or adult acquaintances who are simply in a position to help a teen as a friend or mentor may have a greater impact.

Whether you are a parent, relative, or friend, first suspend your judgments about the teen in question (and teens in general!) and isolate your specific difficulty. Then review the "Seven Ways to Coach Your Teen," and try one simple exercise, or even part of one, to help bridge the gap. Do your part to initiate the healing process.

I feel that I have a long way to go in learning all of this parent-coach technique. It seems overwhelming. Where can I start?

Start with RESPECT; everything falls under the banner of respect, for yourself and others. Consider how you treat a stranger, even a difficult person—an unhappy customer or an unwelcome guest. Then think of how you treat your teenager. Are you at least as polite and respectful as you are with someone whom you don't know?

Review the First Way of coaching teens, by expressing respect. Find one practice exercise that you feel you can manage, and start slowly. Put a sticky note on the fridge or computer that says "respect" so you'll be reminded throughout the day what you are focusing on. Then move into the Seven Ways one at a time, and be patient with yourself and your teen.

NOTES

★

SUCCESS STORIES FROM AROUND THE WORLD

Nothing is more pressing for the well-being of families today than integrating the power and passion of teens. Our future as a society literally depends on it. Diana Sterling is one of the few with a plan for accomplishing it.

Frederick Marx, Director / Writer, Academy Award Nominee for Hoop Dreams

The Parent as Coach Approach® is a handbook with advice and skills to build relationships with our teens. Every parent masters the roles of "Parent as Teacher" & "Parent as Administrator," but as the teenage years arrive our skills turn rusty, our patience level dips, yelling and arguments increase, and the relationship with our children unwinds. Why does this happen? Teenagers are going through a troubling and confusing time, searching for goals, anxious about future decisions, looking for independence, and yearning for acceptance. An administrator is out of a job, and instead a COACH is needed. Thanks to Diana Sterling, there is a solution. To build a healthy and positive parent – teen relationship is a must to provide our children with future possibilities of happiness. For a start, let our teenager know that we love and respect them, their viewpoints, ideas, and interests are important to us.

As we shift from administrator to coach, our vocabulary and tone of voice changes, we begin listening on an altogether different level, open minded and non judgmental, offering deep understanding from their point of view, acknowledging appreciation and giving support. Diana has listed seven commandments, blocks that build upon each ensuring success in showing our child that they are worthy and worthwhile. The cornerstone is RESPECT, which every individual needs and desires. Diana gives advice, pointers and homework ideas to successfully accomplish each step. (I love the yellow sticky papers to remind me to respect, appreciate, support and etc.) The steps continue with LISTEN, UNDERSTAND, APPRECIATE, SUPPORT, RESPONSIBLE and finally INDEPENDENCE. I have begun adapting these steps with my pre-teens and students; slowly a warmer and closer relationship is budding. We have been using the expression "Please keep watering the flowers," or "The flowers need more watering now," when APPRECIATION & RESPECT is waning.

I keep "Parent as Coach" by my bedside as a constant companion.

Sari Bernstein, Brooklyn, New York USA

Thanks to The Parent as Coach Approach, the communication with my daughter is improving. I will continue to use these tips in all my relationships. It was so insightful to meet you. Diana, the world is a better place having you out there. Thank you.

Marie Parkes, Miami, Florida USA

We are a better family for having a coach who is trained in the Parent as Coach Approach. It is the best investment you could do for the ones you love most.

Elena Guardia de Medina, Panama City, Panama

The Parent as Coach Approach has transformed my world. Since learning and applying the approach for the last 5 years my two teenage boys, now 15 & 19, they have grown into wonderfully responsible, caring, confident and independent young men. Instead of dreading the teenage revolution I have thoroughly enjoyed the teenage evolution! The Parent as Coach tools and strategies have also been used widely in all my relationships to wonderful effect. Thank you Diana!

Tracy Tresidder, Sydney, Australia

Diana, I was able to talk to my son Stephen and introduced him to the concept of putting himself in other peoples shoes (he had never been able to do that before.) Thank you for being you and allowing me to be me, even when I did not know who I was.

Carol Shepley, England, UK

I just used the first of the Seven Ways with my son. I told him I respect him for all his hard work at school...and you could hear the excitement in his voice as I recognized his efforts.....YOU HAVE A GOD GIVEN GIFT. Now I am going to praise my wife with lots of respect and listening to her point of view and get in the top 2% group. God bless you!

Seven Days Later

I have been practicing RESPECT and LISTENING deeply in most cases with GREAT results: more interesting conversations, more lively, less of me and more of the TEENS. I have found it takes reprogramming your mind and heart, daily recommitment, and you need to catch yourself preparing to speak negative and redirect for the positive. Since we are never "finished" as parents, adults, workers, husbands, etc. I have also expanded your teaching/guidance to "my contacts beyond teens" to help me in reprogramming myself because practice makes perfect and because the TEENS are the most challenging. I am getting tons of practice with everyone I come in contact with. As a daily reminder I have put Parent as Coach on my daily planner and it helps remind me every time I look at it to be respectful, be positive, be a good listener and brighten up someone's day. God bless you and thanks for the lifetime lesson. PS: My wife and kids and co-workers are grateful.

Frank George, Ft. Lauderdale, Florida, USA

I will take on the Parent as Coach Approach as part of my being, as I believe that the whole philosophy of The Seven Ways is not exclusive to parents, but is how we should treat all others.

Claire Golding, Australia

"The Ryan Story" lives on. No one is happier about that than I am. I strongly believe that I would have lost my son without Diana's approach. If millions of other families are transformed HALF as much as Ryan and I have been over the past six years, the world will be changed beyond comprehension and recognition. I feel honored to be a part of Diana's dream and journey.

Chris Lee, Orlando, Florida USA

From the first time I talked to Diana Sterling I knew this process all began with respect - for myself and modeling for my children (2 daughters). After a few years of this which I continue to grow from, just yesterday I taught my youngest daughter the value of respect and boundaries and supporting versus rescuing. We created an agreement around assisting her in financing her own car. Huge for a kid who expects everything to be handed to her!

Terri Barbato, Philadelphia, Pennsylvania USA

I recently had the experience of helping my daughter move into her dorm room at college. During this trying time I stayed conscious of things I learned from the Parent as Coach Approach. My daughter was very anxious about getting back to school. Her class schedule was still unconfirmed, she had a new roommate, she had a very full class schedule and there were conflicting issues with that schedule. It seemed that everything was happening at once and much was unsettled and unknown for my daughter.

I stayed clear about my role as a coach and did not try to take over and control the situation or rescue my daughter from the inevitable frustration and stress of the situation. I felt the most important thing for me to do was to be supportive and let her be in control. Therefore, I stayed conscious about where she wanted things placed while I helped her unpack and move into her dorm room. I could very easily have told her where I thought things should go and why. But, based on the principles I learned from Parent as Coach, I empowered her to make decisions for herself.

I let her tell me what she wanted to do for lunch. I didn't try to rescue her or think for her. It was important as the "coach" in this situation to continuously acknowledge her for what she was feeling and support her in her in stepping into this time of self-responsibility. As her coach, I simply acknowledged that she would be able to figure it out. I let her talk. I listened. I stayed aware of not telling her how to handle everything that was coming up for her.

I am grateful for my Parent as Coach training that helped me remember how important my role was in this moment to be her coach, not an overprotective hovering mother. I was there to support, offer suggestions, and let her make decisions. Fortunately for me the principles of the Parent as Coach approach were fresh in my mind.

When I left to catch my plane she was peaceful. Her room was unpacked. She'd resolved her class schedule and figured out how to manage her 2 conflicting meetings. I saw her as capable and loved and held space for her to figure it out. And she saw me as supportive and loving. What could have been an antagonizing day of control, turned into one of her transitioning into adult behavior and me getting to witness that and shift along with her to allow it. She is capable.

Eileen Piersa MA, MS. Certified Family Coach, Carlsbad, California USA

When I first came across Diana's material my children were small and WOW! This material has supported me to create an empowering family environment! The approach is easy to understand and implement and works with children of all ages. If you want your home to be a happy place to be and to support your children in a firm, fair and understanding way then this is the material for you. Professionally, The Parent as Coach Approach has influenced and impacted my work in the UK enormously. Her easy to understand approach is transferable to so many different situation and family dynamics. It does what it says on the packet; it supports parents to raise children who are not only well adjusted but compassionate and respectful to themselves first and then the wider society as a whole!

Sarah Newton, #1 Teen Coach in the UK, author of Help! My Teenager is an Alien! Northampton, England, UK

Parent as Coach has provided simple, easy to use tools to help parents of addicts transform the resistant, combative, ineffective relationships they tend to experience into respectful, loving relationships that support recovery rather than addiction. Thanks for making it simple!

Linda Stokes, Director of Services, Parents Helping Parents, Inc., Oklahoma City, OK USA

This model is unique, invaluable, and also "touchable." Anyone could run with it. IT WORKS!

Jaime Simpson, Hong Kong China

After your One-Hour Parent as Coach Approach Seminar I had a fabulous time with both my children on Friday – the same day!

I'm always busy and I love to multitask, believing that I'm getting more bang for my buck with my time. This has, unfortunately, included how I talk to my kids. At some point on Friday, you mentioned letting your kids know how important they are by stopping everything and giving them your undivided attention (very hard for me, that means I'm not doing laundry, dishes and all the other 100's of things that need to be done!), but I tried it anyway. While doing dishes my daughter started talking to me and I stopped and sat down next to her (wow!!!). She looked surprised for a second, then started to smile and continued speaking. When my son got home I tried it with him and he wasn't as easily convinced that I really cared, but when I persisted and took them out to dinner and really listened to them (yes, I put my blackberry in my purse!), they were so animated and even how they related to each other changed. They weren't fighting with each other and whining. So, now that my husband is back from being out of town, I'll have to do some modeling for him to see. Thanks again, and may your program influence the world, beyond your wildest dreams.

Angela Bryan, Miami, Florida USA

Insightful, sound and compassionate, Diana Sterling shows you how to become the parent you have always wanted to be... You must read this book - you can't afford not to.

Fran Rudolph, Family and Life Coach, Parent, North Carolina, USA

The Parent as Coach book is a WHOA! This material and Diana is a gift to this generation.

Chioma Iheukwumere, Nigeria

Joanne, who was formerly as special education student now no longer needs assistance. I am one happy mom who can't say enough about The Parent as Coach Approach.

Lisa Carey, Reston, Virginia USA

I use the Parent as Coach Approach with my own three children and with my clients, communication has dramatically improved and relationships have strengthened. The Parent as Coach Approach brings me closer to my children, while, at the same time, supporting them to develop self-respect, self-confidence, coping skills and independence. Parent as Coach supports my family and other families to thrive and be at our best!

Jane Richards, Certified Family Coach, North Vancouver, British Columbia Canada

I just wanted to thank you for generously sharing your stories and wisdom on raising teens with a coaching perspective. I am a step-mother of two teens, and I look forward to being more of a cheerleader and less of a "nudge" as they navigate through these important years. My step teens thank you, too!

Leslie Leinbach, parent, San Diego, CA USA

Meeting you and learning Parent as Coach has changed my life.

Kristina Dabrowski Haugsand, Sweden

As a parent of teens and a professional coach, I have enjoyed numerous courses in Life Coaching yet Diana's book increased and enriched the foundation of skills I was building on. Parent as Coach 'connected the dots' allowing me to offer more encompassing coaching to both teens and parents. My toolkit is abundant with 'specialty tools' giving me the freedom to make a difference. Thank you Diana!

Helene Illife, parent of teens, Vancouver Canada

What a great approach! Made me really think about some things I'm doing with my 12 year-old daughter, which I can change as she becomes even more of a teenager. Thanks for your time, talent and wisdom.

Denise Ackerman, parent, McKinney, Texas USA

Thanks so much for offering the Parent as Coach approach; there are a number of ideas for me to consider as practices. Our situation is a complex one, and since I am the step-mom, I don't have the "authority" to make a lot of decisions, although I can change my own reactions to Krista. You are doing such important work!!

Joanie Sarin, parent and Career Coach, Phoenix, Arizona USA

The Parent as Coach Approach and The Seven Ways to Coach are the foundation of a high school mentoring/coaching program I helped to create called "Teens as Life-Coaches for Kids." I use this approach in providing skills training to the teens and also in my counseling work with elementary school students. These methods work!

Vicky Martin, Elementary School Counselor, North Clackamas School District, Oregon USA

What an impact this book had on my family's life! As a mother of teens, it empowered me and gave me valuable tools to improve my relationship with my son Scott in his teen years. Thank you.

Susie Samuel, Queens, New York USA

I took away value that I could use immediately with both my 13 and 9 year old. I had a big Aha! and my perspective shifted. I am a marketing professional who has been working with the parents of pre-teens and teens for the last two years. I think your work is breakthrough and I applaud you. I look forward to sharing you and your message with both the parenting and coaching community that I am a part of. We also had a conversation last night about how she hates when she I'm on the phone and she comes in the room and mouths silently to me and I share it very cavalierly with whoever I'm talking to. It was such a very basic issue of respect and I got it. And she got that I got it! Was very good moment.

Saundra Alexis Heath, parent and marketing executive, New York, NY USA

When my friends say, "Just wait until the teen years," in regard to my 9 year old daughter, I say, "Bring it on." The Parent as Coach Approach has greatly improved our communication and I believe the teen years will be a smooth ride for both of us.

Denise Giambalvo, single parent, Portland, OR USA

My wife and I utilize The Parent as Coach Approach all the time and, as a result, our marriage, our family and our four boys are thriving, but, here's the real kicker – I use The Parent as Coach Approach in the workplace too! It is as useful guiding one of my veteran scientists or one of my newly minted managers as it is giving feedback while riding alongside my fifteen year-old son who just got his learner's permit and is sitting behind the wheel of my car! I keep a copy of The Parent as Coach Approach book on my desks at home and at the office and refer to them often.

Dr. Michael R. Klass, Senior Director, Molecular Diagnostics, Ventana Medical Systems Inc., Tucson, Arizona USA

Diana is like a modern day alchemist. She has discovered how to turn coal into gold. As a professional coach I use the Parent as Coach Approach with clients with astounding results. I have witnessed clients take these tools and build a better relationship with the teens in their life.

Christine Santoro, Certified Family Coach, Los Angeles, California USA

I use the Parent as Coach Approach in my classroom as a sixth grade teacher/"parent"/mentor in an inner city immigrant school. My students are learning who they really are, what awesome strengths they possess and most of all what in life they are in control of. They know that they are responsible for their actions, consequences and of course the choices they make as they grow. Being a teacher with the Seven Ways in my pocket makes the entire experience more meaningful, sincere and most of all less stressful. I feel like I am using all I've got to be the best teacher I can be!!

Feigy Myski, teacher, Brooklyn, New York USA

I'd been doing much of The Parent as Coach Approach without knowing what it was for years and because of it, my marriage and my 4 boys are thriving. Now that I've discovered and read Diana Sterling's book and the Seven Ways, I feel both affirmed and better equipped as a wife, mother, coach and business woman. Diana's work provides the language and skills required to parent well in the 21st Century and, even more important, because her work helped me to better understand, organize and articulate what I was doing, I've been able to share my knowledge and teach my husband, my children and my clients the Seven Ways. I see them applying these skills in their lives and relationships and as a result, they know, first hand, that it works. My kids tell me over and over that they love it that I'm a coach! Now, every mom and dad can acquire these skills, apply them immediately and become more effective in all of their roles. I promise you, this will change your life, your kid's life and the world for the better.

Dori Klass, Adult & Teen Advocate, Executive Coach & Leadership Consultant, Tucson, Arizona USA

As a mother of two, I have experienced the benefits of Diana Sterling's wisdom when it comes from interaction with children and approaching them with deep listening, respect, love and clear requests. The Parent as Coach Approach is personal, practical and offers sage advice for building a strong foundation with your beloved children, as well as all others near and dear to your hear.

Teddy Berney, parent, Beaverton, Oregon USA

Parent as Coach taught me the power of telling my children what I see in them. I have only told my children (ages 5 and under) a few times to their faces that they were each amazing, but the evidence that they internalized this message was clear as day when my 5 year-old son was at the doctor's office one day, and as they were measuring him for height, weight, etc., he straightened himself up, looked the nurse straight in the eye and stated: "I am amazing." He knows it and is not ashamed to tell it to the world!

Janette Sassoon, LMSW, Brooklyn, New York USA

Thank you for your perspective and tools of Parent as Coach. I think the thing that has helped the most is the change in perspective I've had.

Judy Bouton, Parent, Portland, Oregon USA

The Parent as Coach Approach has become, in large part, the foundation piece I use when coaching parents, helping them to become the coach in their teens' lives. It is easy to read, understand, and comprehend, and is a great tool for coaches and parents. I highly recommend it to anyone coaching parents and teens.

Isabelle Zehnder, Certified Family Coach, Vancouver, Washington USA

Mom listens better than she did before the coaching. She is also getting better at supporting me. I also think Mom has helped me become more independent. Overall I think Mom has improved over the last four months and that she should continue to work on this.

Joanne Carey, 13 years old, Reston, VA USA

The Parent as Coach Approach works for me, for all ages from 5 on up!! I have used the Seven Ways over and over again, they work every time! We teach our children to respect us and themselves. This book reminds us that RESPECT might mean something to us, but it needs to be defined for our children the way we think it, the way we hear it, the way we see it. Look out for the fabulous adventure of rediscovering your child with each of the seven ways!! AND, the child discovering their parent!

Dara Stieglitz, parent and Certified Success Coach, New Jersey, USA

Parent as Coach found my husband and me just in time – before our oldest turned 13. Now it is our anchor, helping us weather the storms of mood swings, and not get lost in the sea of teen angst. Parent as Coach can help you, too, deepen and strengthen your relationship with your children well into the teen years, and beyond.

Venus Taylor, homeschooling mother of 2, Boston, Mass. USA

As I reflect upon The Parent as Coach Approach, I know that perfection is not the goal, connection is. It all begins with respect and keeping the emphasis on your teen, not yourself. Compassionate understanding is the key.

Becky Thompson, Farmington, New Mexico USA

"Way to go, mom. I love you."

Jordan Haskins

Send us YOUR success story and we will feature you and your family in our next book.

Email us at support@parentascoach.com.

ORI'S STORY

...you know that feeling, your innocent child reminds you of a brewing thunderstorm, you are aware that the sweet days are counted and your defenses are down to a thin thread where rupture and eruptions seems to be the only option.

I was not sure what I have in front of me, a teenager testing the grounds or something much more complex. Four years later clear green eyes looked into mine and my son gave me the most unexpected and beautiful compliment: "Where would I be without you, Mom?"

Complex he was - my, our Ori (hebrew 'My Light') was an emergency premie with an early diagnosis of hydrocephalus, (excess water on the brain) which had to be shunted when he was just 3 weeks into his tiny life.

My husband, a musician and I, a painter decided to never be for one second without one another and so Ori traveled with us from concert to concert around the world. A healthy looking, friendly baby shone every day at us and with his hospitalization background in mind, we did not expect wonders in fast development.

After a year the little pump in his head quit working and he needed another one.

He was a pale and sick, thin little boy for weeks, but then he started to blossom. He walked, he ate, he sang, he painted, he laughed, he swung through the next 4 years always a little awkward and slow but with great surprises up his sleeve. He kept his development secret 'til the last moment and then suddenly decided to come up with new skills, surprising thoughts well expressed, humorous remarks beyond his tender age and interests of great intensity that seem to be a must-do-and-have, like collecting airplane safety instruction cards. We loved the slower pace he took, it seemed like nature was thoughtful with our son. Traveling so much we were not sure where exactly Ori stood in comparison to other children. He had been almost exclusively with adults, never seemed to miss other children - we wanted him to socially catch up and needed to know where he stood.

A top-notch child university psychology department gave us a devastating answer: Ori would not develop any further, his delays are great and he doesn't seem to understand things, so there must be retardation progressing and we were advised to prepare for an uncertain future.

Stunned, we decided that we know better. Our child had enjoyed the world of Mozart and Brahms, had a light but strongly contoured personality and to us he was very bright. We had settled in Central Florida, still traveling a lot, but for Ori, I stayed more often at home so that he could visit pre-school and sing in the church children's choir. A new baby was under way. Ori was angry and jealous, a fact he never forgot and as the child died in his ninth month inside of me he felt responsible for his little brother's passing.

The search for a school in our area was a failure. Knowing Ori was kind-of unprepared, I had taken him to an occupational therapist with very mixed results.

Again, Ori was not ready for school according to the therapist, but time was running out as he was almost seven. Then the public school system opened the door for us and from then on Ori progressed. He loved to be around children, he decided to read and write from one day to another and he was well liked by teachers because he was such an interesting child with many entertaining experiences other children did not have and he was funny. Another shunt operation stopped him for a short period of time. He took it as a fact of life and wanted nothing more than to be back in school. In fourth grade he got teased for the first time and took it very personally. It became clear that he did not connect socially in a satisfying way; not making friends as he could not read the gestures and expressions of others. Being comfortable alone, he watched TV and read. Oddly, his TV watching was not for fun. It looked very much like he was studying – and learning.

His school performance became uneven, his concept understanding showed as being fragmented. Still, Ori had almost completely straight A's because of fabulous memory skills that got him out of traps easily. A history buff and walking lexicon he passionately hated questions which made it quite difficult to keep him integrated in the mainstream classes. His 'concrete thinking' started to stand in his way and the class pace was often too fast to give him time to sort his sophisticated vocabulary for correct responses. He made adjustments. As an example he developed a unique way of writing that allowed him speed and therefore support for comprehension.

Then I heard for the first time about Asperger's Syndrom. Our son was a perfect match. Ori himself was right on the mark, he knew precisely the differences between himself and others but could not change them. He identified himself perfectly as not being imaginative, not understanding broad concepts but to his frustration he could not create the links. He loved his peers but could not connect enough to get friendship in return.

At home he kept increasingly to himself and insisted on privacy while having vast conversations with himself or listening to classical music. He asked for some homework help which he governed in an unpleasant defensive way. He was a teenager alright.

At thirteen Ori had a first seizure and our journey through doctor's offices and medication began. He took the new circumstance practical in a way – the word 'burden' did not exist for him. Despite this, he loved fishing, theatre, cooking and passionately the people associated with these activities – the many teachers he picked with certainty.

Within a short time hostility between the unprepared me and the defensive him grew into a looming concern. In school he made an overwhelming effort to stay afloat, at home he let go of all inhibitions and fought me with rejection and disrespect. His father being away often. With a mind focus on literature, music and himself, with grandparents who adhered to a traditional concept of upbringing with punishment in the center, I quickly stood in front of a wall with big letters written on it: You cannot let this child treat you like this - he will become a victim of himself!

I had long begun to built up expertise about all of Ori's conditions and anticonvulsant medications and was highly suspicious about the effects laid on Ori's psyche. I came to the conclusion

that I need both, advice how to answer to his aggression and a
continuous search for the right medication and doctor.

"Parent as Coach" spoke to me immediately as I searched
the internet. I found Diana. This was what I needed; a coach, a
guide and I made contact. We agreed on regular telephone conversations. Her background as a mother, a creative film maker, a
former management trainer was convincing enough to keep me
interested in what she would have to say and soon I could not
wait to hear her singing voice telling me the truth. Over the next
months she coached me into the meaning of words that are so easily used in everyday language, their connection and their appli-
cation and the effect of their use: Respect; Listen; Understand;
Appreciate; Support; Responsible; Independence; Love.

I will never forget how Ori perked up when he heard me say
that I respect what he has to say and who he is. The glow of trust
when he noticed that I was truly listening to him, patiently and
with my full attention to the content 'between the lines' was a
priceless expression. The magic began to work both ways the
more Diana lifted my awareness toward my own actions, my
thoughts, my planning, my life and toward Ori's inner life. The
process translated in great changes in the quality, length and content of conversations between Ori and me. Not long and WE were
growing. The effects paid everywhere as multi-way streets. My
engagement in Ori's school was well respected and desired, the
teens in his theater club took me serious as a medium between
him and them, we became a strong and liked character-pair
going to restaurants or showing up at ball games. Ori wanted
me to be everywhere with him so that he can communicate better and I took the role with pleasure. He taught me about how
much independence he needs and I happily stood back. He took
his responsibilities very serious and no one doubted this. And he
was always comfortable and forceful to work with me through
difficult issues.

Yes, we fought despite the bliss. He truly learned that I am
human too and knew now that he had always been surrounded by
an abundance of love and care. And not one day came to a conclusion before its problems were resolved.

Diana's infusion of life lessons, well studied, sensibly analyzed and placed was bearing fruit in peace of mind for both of us and no fear clouded what the future might hold. Ori's main concern was not to be misunderstood and we kept working on clarity with great intensity.

The past four years since the first conversation with Diana shine on for both Ori and me in a very special, dense light. Ori passed away at the age of 17 during an epilepsy episode on March 28, 2008. About a thousand people said good bye to him at his funeral service at our little town's public park, each of them not only with fond memories in their hearts but the knowledge that respect is the key to ones who are different among us.

I thank Diana for the great gift of having learned to appreciate my child and having had the privilege to be appreciated by this precious, beautiful son, who said to me in his final days,

"Where would I be without you, Mom?"

"You are my Light, Ori!"

ABOUT THE AUTHOR: DIANA STERLING

DIANA STERLING

CEO, Parent, Coach and author of The Parent as Coach Approach

Diana Sterling (formerly Diana Haskins) is a 30-year veteran business owner and innovator. Her commitment to helping others find meaning and success has resulted in the creation of New Generations International, Inc., a personal and professional development company serving teens, young adults, parents, families and individuals worldwide.

As CEO, Diana oversees three divisions of New Generations International. Her fantastically effective business educational program, *Vision in Action* is a testimony for her relentless enthusiasm for self-employment, which she founded on the heels of her transformation from Film Production Company owner to New Generations International CEO. The second division *Parent as Coach*, is a series of programs designed to support parents going through the struggling teen years of parenting. Diana and her son Jordan, now 24, found that the skills and systems of coaching allowed them both to migrate successfully through his often difficult teen years and her even more difficult "parent of teen" years. *The Academy for Family Coach Training* is the third division and complements the other two by offering the world acclaimed Advanced Coaching Course, which trains professionals in the art of professional coaching in the specialty of teens, young adults, parents and families.

In addition to her leadership role, Diana is an executive coach, public speaker, trainer and facilitator in the areas of Small Business Development, Parenting, Life Skills for Youth, and Professional Coaching. She has a wealth of knowledge and communicative skills acquired through her background in coaching, teaching, drama, music and film production. Diana holds a Bachelor Degree in Drama and is working towards a Masters Degree in Education majoring in Adult Learning and Development at Portland State University. She has completed a Professional Certificate in Coaching at New Ventures West and holds the distinction of being a Neuro-Linguistic Programming Practitioner, certified by Life Design International.

Diana is an avid reader and student of philosophy, world religions, intercultural communication and history.

Diana is the author of The Parent as Coach Approach: The Seven Ways to Coach Your Teen in the Game of Life (White Oak Publishing 2008), which has international distribution in North America, Latin America, Korea, Europe and Australia and has been translated into Spanish and Korean. She is a member of the International Coach Federation and the International Speakers Network. Diana is known for her innovative and creative style of coaching and training having achieved excellent results with a diverse base of individual clients, including corporate executives, small business owners, service professionals, professional coaches, parents and teenagers.

Prior to founding New Generations International, Diana served as Executive Producer of The Production Team, Inc, which she founded in 1993. She is an award winning film and video producer with over fifteen years as a freelance producer. She produced and directed a thirty-minute documentary, "Guerilla Theatre" for Outside In, a non-profit agency working with homeless youth, earning her a First Place Telly Award, which took her deep into the world of homeless youth. This has become a moving reminder to help others, more importantly young people.

Diana is a Body for Life 2002 Winner in Bill Phillips Body for Life worldwide competition, completing a 12-Week body overhaul challenge on her 45th birthday. She is featured in *Body for Life for Women*. Diana is also a featured contributor to *Wake Up... Live The Life You Love; The Power of Team* along with Dr. Wayne Dyer and Tony Robbins.

Diana is known for her unique blend of education and entertainment in both presentation and curriculum design and her enthusiasm for helping people is infectious. Diana is married to a caring, insightful man of God, Bill Sterling, adding to her growth on a daily basis. And the true inspiration for her dedication to young people comes from her positive relationship with her grown son, Jordan, who says on a regular basis, "Go for it, Mom!"

ABOUT NEW GENERATIONS INTERNATIONAL

New Generations International is a global-reaching professional and personal growth coaching, training and publishing company. We offer a powerful combination of live seminars, teleseminars, individual and group coaching and products: books, e-books, audio books, DVD's, CD's and workbooks. We promote healthy communication, self-confidence, courage and personal and financial responsibility for self, community and the planet through the attainment of self awareness and higher consciousness. We embrace all traditions of culture, faith and family. We are based in Albuquerque, New Mexico.

We believe that all people are entitled to explosive personal growth and remarkable discovery of their full potential. From this philosophy we are committed to delivering programs to teenagers, young adults, parents and families. We believe that the family is the personal and social foundation for success in life as well as the root of all healthy relationships. We are supporting new generations of potential, love, growth and insight. Our diverse offerings are headed under three separate divisions; Vision in Action, Academy for Family Coach Training and Parent as Coach.

RECOMMENDED RESOURCES

PARENT AS COACH®
www.parentascoach.com

*The Parent as Coach Approach Audio Book
CD or Download to your MP3*

*The Parent as Coach DVD Live workshop filmed
with Diana Sterling*

Spanish Version of Parent as Coach

The Parent as Coach® coaching and training philosophy is based on the belief that we first need to understand what human beings are in order to teach and coach them. This includes often misunderstood teens! From this place of understanding, we learn to offer support, ideas, new perspectives, plans for moving forward, and a host of tools and formats to help people create fulfilling and meaningful lives. Above all, we offer love and compassion to all we serve and come in contact with.

Our approach is a proven and practical model for improving and transforming the relationship we as adults have with the teens in our lives. It is based on the roots and synthesis of life coaching, adult learning theories, positive psychology, child development theories, adolescent development, and education and mentoring.

To receive discounts for ordering books and materials in large quantities, please call us at 505-247-2902.

ACADEMY FOR FAMILY COACH TRAINING
www.familycoachtraining.com

Advanced Coaching Course (10 months);
become a Certified Family Coach

12 Week Custom Coaching Program for Professionals

4 Week Teleseminar

Is your purpose to heal, support and guide young people and their parents in creating loving and productive lives? Our programs are accredited with **the International Coach Federation as an ACSTH Accredited Program as well as Lewis and Clark College with the Masters Degree CEU designation**. We are the only fully comprehensive coach training academy in the world for professionals who work with teens, young adults, parents and families. Join us in making a difference in your country, community and family.

The Academy for Family Coach Training has developed truly unique training and coaching offering that no other company can match because it consists of a series of proven techniques that condense over 30 years of collective coaching, education and training experience into a proven system for working professionally with teens, young adults, parents and family groups. The Academy for Family Coach Training is committed to establishing and expanding successful partnerships between teens, young adults, parents, families, and the professionals who support them. Our Certified Family Coaches teach and coach teens, young adults, parents and family groups how they can have incredible, connected and powerful communication in their families. Where there may be stress, lack of harmony, conflict and despair, we deliver hope!

VISION IN ACTION
www.visioninaction.com

Vision in Action DVD Home Learning Course

Vision in Action 3 Day Training

Vision in Action Coaching Program

Moms, dads, parents, families and young people! Do you have an entrepreneurial spirit? Vision in Action Training and Coaching Programs provide you with the structure, curriculum and accountability you require to take your small business to the next level. The outcome? Your business will function in a logical, efficient, and unified manner, paced to create REAL results. You will become aligned with your Vision in Action, not left wandering about in your dreams. Exactly how does this happen? We will be your guides as you create and implement a strategic plan designed to dramatically improve your business and your life. Get ready to get the lead out!

SPEAKING ENGAGEMENTS
www.dianasterling.com

Diana Sterling has been referred to as having a "quiet potency in public speaking." Her easy and sincere approach is balanced with finesse, care and enthusiasm. Her message conveys a perfect blend of everyday solutions with uncommon wisdom. Audiences take home something that they can implement that very day, causing them to say, "This works!" To have Diana Sterling present at your next event, email diana@dianasterling.com or call 1-505-247-2902.

HOW TO REACH US

Diana Sterling
White Oak Publishing
New Generations International
4111 Barbara Loop SE, Suite E-1
Rio Rancho, New Mexico 87124
USA

Ph. (505) 247-2902
support@parentascoach.com

On the Web:
www.parentascoach.com
www.dianasterling.com
www.visioninaction.com
www.familycoachtraining.com

WITH GRATITUDE

Without a doubt, *Parent as Coach* would not have been possible without my "fine young son," Jordan Haskins. He is my teacher, my inspiration, and my daily reminder of what's really important. Thank you for coming into my life, Jordan. To bring this message and this important work forward, my heart is deeply appreciative to my husband Bill Sterling, my *"emotional support, baby!"*

Sincere appreciation goes to Machele Brass who has so beautifully enhanced the words with her fine graphics. And to my great friend Kal Yee, photographer and creative director extraordinaire! My thanks to Jean Staeheli for her unconditional love, editorial guidance, and support for the idea of *Parent as Coach*; and to Nancy Osa, a brilliant and wonderful woman and editor, without whom there would be no book.

I am grateful for the leadership and teaching of my original coaching trainer James Flaherty, author of *Coaching: Evoking Excellence in Others* and founder of New Ventures West. And I am profoundly thankful to Lynda Falkenstein, author of *Nichecraft*, for her wise counsel, supportive mentorship, and strategy which had brought us here to this point.

Humble thanks go to all of the parents, young people, coaches, trainers, friends and authors who have contributed to my growth as a leader, parent and a coach-whose collective wisdom is contained in my heart and here in these pages. This book is a team effort by our devoted staff at New Generations International and our industry leaders in coaching, training and personal development.

Finally, a reverent thank-you to my own parents, William "Pop" Hicks and Evelyn Hicks. Without their support and love, indeed, I could not have created the idea of *The Parent as Coach Approach*.

Diana Sterling
Albuquerque, New Mexico USA

NOTES

★

NOTES

★

NOTES

★